GIFTS FROM YOUR GARDEN

By the same authors:
Gifts from the Kitchen

Other books by Joan Scobey:
Rugs & Wall Hangings
Celebrity Needlepoint
Do-It-All-Yourself Needlepoint

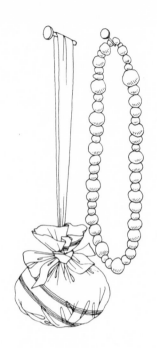

GIFTS
FROM YOUR
GARDEN

by JOAN SCOBEY
and NORMA MYERS

Illustrations by Paul Bacon

BOBBS-MERRILL   *Indianapolis / New York*

All rights reserved including the right of reproduction
in whole or in part in any form
Published by The Bobbs-Merrill Company, Inc.
Indianapolis / New York

ISBN 0-672-51895-3 Hardcover
Library of Congress Catalog Card Number: 75-512
Designed by Helen Barrow
Manufactured in the United States of America

First printing

Library of Congress Cataloging in Publication Data

Scobey, Joan.
    Gifts from your garden.

    Includes index.
    1. Gardening. 2. Handicraft. 3. Gifts.
I. Myers, Norma, joint author. II. Title.
SB454.S38   745.92   75-512
ISBN 0-672-51895-3

TO OUR RUTHIE
who loves all growing things

ACKNOWLEDGMENTS

Gardeners have always been gift-givers, finding the worthiest presents in the soil around them. We are grateful to many old and new friends among them who generously and enthusiastically shared their crops and their crafts with us:

    Suzanne Cherbuliez
    Gordon Garnett
    Harriet Kapel
    Ellin London
    Mrs. Katherine Macy
    Kay McCahan
    Roberta Moffitt
    Frances Numrich
    Adelma Simmons and Doris Civitello, Caprilands Herb Farm
    Harriet Sobol
    Esther Shay
    Ann Spindel

    and most particularly to Marybeth Weston, who has always had a green thumb with friends as well as with plants,

    and to Wendy Myers and Rick Scobey for their editorial and research contributions.

CONTENTS

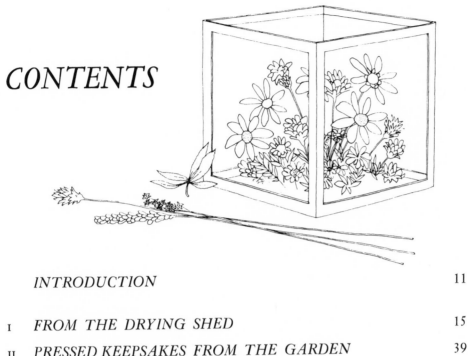

INTRODUCTION

In Persia during the sixth century there lived a king, Chosroes I, who greatly delighted in his gardens. Saddened when the harsh winds of winter drove him indoors away from his beloved blooms, he ordered an immense carpet made. It was about ninety feet square, woven in silk and encrusted with gemstones to represent the flowers and canals of an actual park. He laid this carpet of legendary beauty, which came to be called "The Spring of Chosroes," on the palace floor where it became his indoor garden, extending the verdant joys of spring and summer throughout the year.

This yearning for everlasting bloom strikes commoner as well as king, for inevitably the seasons change. The exuberant growth of spring becomes the harvest of autumn or dies away to renew itself for spring again. Not many among us can command a bejewelled carpet to keep the glories of the garden ever with us, but we can preserve its fruits in many marvelous ways to enjoy in other seasons. In a sense, this book is meant to be a magic carpet, helping you prolong the pleasures of your garden.

Whereas "The Spring of Chosroes" was primarily a joy for the eyes, our gifts from the garden appeal to the other senses as well. They come in many forms—tasty delectations from the flower bed and herb garden; evocative fragrances in sachets, pomanders, fireplace faggots; pressed as botanical compositions and other keepsakes; preserved year round in charming bouquets.

Moreover, gifts from the garden can be made by anyone, whether tending a window sill planter or gardening under lights in the city, tilling a country acre, weeding a suburban plot, or merely roaming a field of wildflowers. We assume you already have a garden, no matter how modest, or can easily find your way to some plants you can legally claim as your own.

As you can see, this is more a book on garden craft than on gardening. In it you will find what to make of garden bounty, how to make it, and how to share it with friends. Some of the required skills are easily mastered, others call for more patience, but all offer great satisfactions. To help you utilize this expertise, you will also find gifts for all seasons and occasions, a timetable for garden giving, and sources of supplies.

We hope this book will lead you into new perceptions of your garden, not only of the momentary pleasures it provides but also of the gift-giving possibilities it promises. We invite you to discover the two-fold joys of gifts from the garden: the growth and renewal that is the wonder of nature, and the sharing of its harvest that is a pleasure of friendship.

JOAN SCOBEY
NORMA MYERS

Flowers . . . are always fit presents
. . . because they are a proud asser-
tion that a ray of beauty outvalues
all the utilities of the world.
RALPH WALDO EMERSON, "Gifts"
Essays: Second Series

I

FROM THE DRYING SHED

Drying flowers and foliage whole—three-dimensionally—is the most lifelike way to recall the growing plants. Stripped though they are of moisture, and sometimes of fragrance, many plants preserved in this way can appear breathtakingly realistic. So if you delight in floral bouquets and arrangements, either for yourself or to present to friends, the techniques of the "drying shed" will most happily extend your garden pleasures year round.

There are two principal ways of drying botanicals, both of which actually remove all moisture from the plant material. The traditional method, practiced at least since colonial times, is air drying, the process of simply exposing plants to circulating air. In general, it is suitable for many wildflowers, grasses, weeds, pods and other plants that flourish in dry sandy soil and in the fields. A newer and quicker method employs desiccants, or drying agents, to speed up dehydration. This method is particularly useful for cultivated flowers that hold too much moisture to be fully dried by air or at least to retain any semblance of their former selves if they could survive the natural air drying process. And because the faster the drying process the better the color retention, desiccants best preserve the carefully cultivated colors and forms of garden specimens.

Your choice of drying method will depend primarily on the plants to be preserved, but you may want to consider other factors as well. Air drying is cheaper, easier, and requires less space or equipment. The plants which dry at a slow natural pace are sturdier than those dried more quickly in desiccants and are often more suitable in informal natural arrangements. Desiccant-dried flowers are more dramatic and reminiscent of the garden, quite fragile, and more suitable to formal floral arrangements.

Plants are living organisms, no more predictable than the weather or obedient to rules of behavior than the rest of us, so if any flower or plant does not dry well by the suggested method, try an alternative. And by all means, experiment with all your favorite plants—flower pods, grains, branches or berries, the flowers of herbs or vegetables, a perfect hybrid blossom—even if they are not specifically listed.

HARVESTING THE FLOWER CROP

Whichever method of preservation you choose, pick your flowers when they look their very best. For most flowers, this will be just at the peak of their bloom when they are not yet so full blown that the petals are about to fall off. For the most interesting arrangements, pick flowers in all stages of their development—as buds and partially open blooms as well as in full flower.

Harvest after the dew has dried, when there is no trace of moisture on the blossoms. If you must gather them when they are wet —at the start of a storm, perhaps, which you fear may decimate the blooms—let the petals dry completely before processing them, meanwhile keeping their stems immersed in warm water.

If it is impossible to process your flowers immediately—ideally, not more than four or five minutes should elapse between picking and preserving—strip them of their leaves and stand their stems in warm water, taking care to keep their petals dry. If flowers wilt during their trip from garden to workroom, plunge their stems into warm tap water and set them in a dark place until they regain their freshness. If there are any flowers you cannot revive, discard them; wilted flowers should not be processed.

AIR DRYING

The simplest method of preserving plants and flowers is by air drying, and the easiest way of doing that is to hang bunches of the plants upside down so their moisture will be absorbed by the circulating air.

You can dry some plants like strawflowers just by standing them upright in a vase.

First strip the leaves from the stems of the plants you want to dry, then gather half a dozen or so in a bunch. Secure their ends in an elastic band which will contract and hold the stems as they dry and shrink. Tie two or three bunches to a wire coat hanger, making sure the hanging flower heads don't touch. Place the coat hangers on nails or along a clothesline in a dry airy room. Avoid hot airless attics and closets, and damp basements. Spread the floor with newspapers to catch any shedding from the drying plants.

The flowers will take anywhere from a few days to two weeks to dry, depending on their density and moistness and the humidity in the air. Take them down as they dry—they will not all dry at the same rate—and store them in containers away from direct sunlight and dampness.

STORAGE. Since you should not assemble any dried arrangements until the weather is dry or the heat in your home is turned on, you may have to store your dried plants for some time. If your storage area is dusty, protect the plants with a paper bag; at this point don't use a plastic bag which might retain some dampness.

PLANTS FOR AIR DRYING. Plants that grow in sandy or poor soil are best for air drying. In general, they are wildflowers, grasses, weeds and pods rather than most cultivated flowers. The following list, though necessarily incomplete, contains well known plants for air drying. They are listed under their most familiar names.

acacia
acroclinium (helipterum)
ageratum
allium
anthurium leaves
armeria (thrift, sea pink)
artemisia (wormwood)
baby's breath
bayberry
bells of Ireland
bittersweet
bridal wreath
broom
buckeye
canna leaves
catalpa pods
cattail
chestnut tree burrs

Chinese lantern
cockscomb (celosia)
daisy
delphinium pods
dock
dusty miller
eucalyptus leaves
gladiolus leaves
globe amaranth (clover flower)
globe thistle (echinops)
goldenrod
grasses
greenbrier or catbrier
heather
honesty (silver dollar, lunaria)
honey locust pods
horse chestnut tree burrs
hydrangea (green, white-pink)
iris pods
Joe-Pye weed
lady's thumb
lamb's ears
larkspur pods
lavender
liatris (button snakeroot)
lotus pods
love-in-a-mist pods
magnolia foliage
milkweed pods
mimosa pods

mountain sage
mullein (verbascum)
nandina berries
oak leaves
palm foliage
pearly everlasting
pennyroyal
poppy pods
pussywillow
pyracantha berries
Queen Anne's lace
redbud (Judas tree)
rose of Sharon pods
sagebrush
salvia farinacea (blue)
sea lavender
silver tree leaves
snapdragon pods
statice
strawflower
sumac foliage and berries
tamarisk
tansy
teasel
wheat
wild bergamot
xeranthemum
yarrow
yucca pods

DRYING AGENTS OR DESICCANTS

Various drying agents can speed the dehydration process from weeks to days. These desiccants are particularly valuable when used with cultivated flowers because the quicker the drying process the better the color retention of the bloom. In the past, sand, white cornmeal and borax have functioned successfully as dehydrating mediums (in the ratio of one part sand or cornmeal to two parts borax), but the chemical silica gel is now widely preferred because of its efficiency and ease of handling. It is the quickest drying agent, it is ready for use without sterilizing, sifting, cleaning, drying or mixing, and although its initial cost is high, it can easily be revived for reuse.

Silica gel is sold commercially under many names, including Petalast and Flower-Dri. Its highly absorbent crystals remain dry to the touch even when it has reached its maximum absorption level. For this reason its white crystals are mixed with blue specks which lose their color as the silica gel absorbs moisture. When no tell-tale blue remains, dry the mixture out for about an hour in a warm oven (no more than 250° F.) until the reappearance of the blue specks indicates the silica gel is ready for reuse.

Even with the help of drying agents there is no promise of true color fidelity. Some flowers retain their original color vividly, others do not; many fade after drying, some more quickly than others, especially in direct sunlight. White flowers often turn cream colored when dried but a few—candytuft, feverfew—appear snow white. The reds of zinnias and roses often darken to purple, blue-red turns cherry, and rose shades become several tones darker. Orange roses become pure red while orange zinnias will probably remain orange. In general, a newly opened flower will hold its color better than one in bloom for a day or two; the older the flower the less likely it is to retain its original color and shape. So work quickly with young, fresh and perfect blooms and the results will delight and perhaps surprise you.

PREPARING THE FLOWERS. As with other drying methods, the key to success is how quickly the flowers can be processed after cutting. Naturally, the flowers should be fresh and just at their prime. Be particularly careful that the petals are completely dry; if they are at all moist they will dry with an unnatural transparency.

When possible, cut the stems to no more than one inch long and remove any remaining foliage. Obviously, long flower stalks like delphinium and larkspur and snapdragon cannot be cut; their florets will be dried while on the stem. Stiffen cut stems with florist wire, using a gauge appropriate to the thickness of the stem and the weight of the flower head. Numbers 18, 20, and 22 are general purpose sizes, available at florists and hobby shops.

Wire the flower stems carefully to avoid damaging the form and petals of the flower head. If the flower has a deep calyx or a thick base, wire around or through it. If the flower has an eye, like a daisy, hook the end of a wire and poke it down through the eye into the cut stem; if you haven't caught the center of the stem, twist the protruding wire around it for support. A few flowers, like pansies, are best wired through the stem first, coming up to the bloom.

DRYING THE FLOWERS. Process flowers in boxes with sides at least an inch higher than the tops of the flowers and with tightly fitting lids. Shoe boxes, plastic and tin storage boxes are excellent.

Most flowers will dry face up. Place at least an inch of silica gel in the bottom of the drying box and set the flower heads in it, bending their wires horizontally out of the way. Be sure the flowers do not touch each other or the sides of the box. Carefully sprinkle silica gel under, around, and between the flower petals, and especially into the center of the flower which holds the most moisture. Cover the box and seal the lid with masking tape, if necessary, to exclude all moisture.

A few flat-petaled flowers like pansies and daisies can be dried face down on a thin bed of silica gel. Sprinkle the absorbent crystals carefully around the petals. You may have to bend the wire stems out of the way to close the box.

Long flower spikes like delphinium, larkspur, and snapdragon that can't be dried face up or upside down are laid on their sides in long boxes on a thin bed of silica gel. To avoid crushing the florets, prop up heavy stalks with cardboard "bridges." Arrange their petals carefully and sprinkle well with silica gel.

Label and date each box of drying flowers, noting both the dates on which the process began and on which it is expected to end. To save space, you can dry in the same box varieties of flowers that require the same drying period.

Drying time varies with different flowers, with the size and condition of the flower when picked, and with the general atmospheric conditions of the drying room. Too short a drying period leaves the flowers limp, too long makes them brittle and apt to shatter. They will have the pleasant rustle of silk taffeta when properly dried.

In general, flowers require three to seven days, the larger and denser blossoms taking the longer time. Follow the drying times recommended by the manufacturer of the silica gel or the information listed on pages 29 to 30, under "Plants for processing in silica gel." If in doubt about the dryness of your flowers during processing, test them after two days and daily thereafter, pushing away enough silica gel to touch the outer petals carefully with a finger. If they feel dry, remove the flowers gently; they are extremely fragile at this stage. Shake the desiccant off the petals and out of the centers lightly, dusting off any clinging granules with a soft camel's hair paint brush.

With a few flowers, especially roses, you will find that the calyxes or centers may still be a little damp and spongy even though the outer petals are dry and crisp. These will require additional drying of the still-moist section without further drying of the petals. To do this, place about half an inch of silica gel on the bottom of a drying box and set each calyx in it firmly, taking care that the petals do not touch the desiccant. Close the box tightly and let the flowers dry for another three or more days. This "outside drying" will be completed when the center feels firm and hard. Be sure the entire flower is completely dry; even the slightest moisture may later turn the flower limp and colorless.

After the flower heads have completely dried, you can give them added stability by running a thin ribbon of glue, such as Duco household cement, around the undersides of each petal and where the petals join the stem or center. You can also glue broken petals back onto the flower.

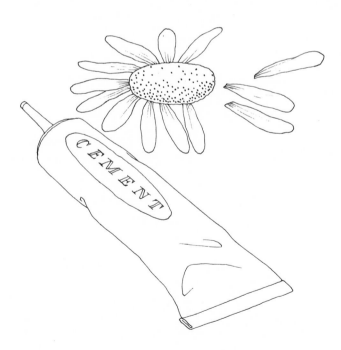

You can prevent further reabsorption of moisture by spraying the dried flowers with a moisture-proofing liquid such as crystal clear Krylon or clear unscented hair spray. Work in a well-ventilated room and apply two light coats of lacquer.

STORAGE. Keep whole dried flowers in a dry place away from dampness, direct sunlight and intense heat. You can hang them carefully or stick their wire stems into blocks of Styrofoam. If your storage area is dusty, cover the flowers gently with a cloth or with paper bags. If it is at all damp, place the dried flowers in storage boxes or plastic bags to which half a cup of silica gel has been added.

If your dried flowers have already been made up in an arrangement, don't dismember it for storage, but do lengthen its life by putting it away through the humid season. Store it in a large box, anchoring the bowl firmly so the flowers don't touch the sides. Add a little silica gel and seal tightly. As an added safeguard in particularly damp climates, pack the box in a large plastic cleaning bag.

PLANTS FOR PROCESSING IN SILICA GEL. Following is a list of flowers that can be preserved in silica gel and their approximate processing times. A few of them require additional drying time, as described above, outside their initial silica immersion. This is noted as "outside drying" in the list below. Most desiccant manufacturers furnish precise information for their own products. The list, although necessarily incomplete, contains well known plants to preserve in silica gel. They are listed under their most familiar names.

acacia	3–4 days
ageratum	3 days
anemone	3 days + outside drying
aster	4–5 days
astilbe	5 days + outside drying
bachelor's button	3 days
bells of Ireland	3–4 days + outside drying
calendula	5–7 days + outside drying
camelia	5 days
candytuft	2–3 days
Canterbury bells	4 days
carnations	4 days
caryopteris	3 days
columbine	4–5 days
coral bells	3 days
cosmos	4–5 days
dahlia	5–7 days
daisy types (painted, oxeye, etc.)	3–5 days
delphinium florets	5–7 days + outside drying
deutzia	2–3 days
dusty miller	5 days

feverfew	5 days
hellebore (Christmas rose)	4 days
hollyhock	4 days
hydrangea (blue, white)	4–5 days
ivy	4 days
lamb's ears	4 days
larkspur	5 days
laurel	4–5 days
lilac	6–7 days
lily of the valley	3 days + outside drying
marigolds	5–7 days + outside drying
pansy	3 days
peonies	4–5 days + outside drying
roses (flowers and foliage)	5–7 days + outside drying
salvia farinacea (blue)	3–4 days
scabiosa	3 days
scilla (wood hyacinth)	4 days + outside drying
snapdragon	5 days + outside drying
snow-on-the-mountain	3–4 days
sweet pea	4–5 days
tithonia (Mexican sunflower)	3 days
verbena	3–4 days
violas, violets, Johnny-jump-ups	2–3 days
violet leaves	4 days + outside drying
zinnias	4–5 days

GLYCERINE TREATMENT FOR LEAVES

Preserved leaves are welcome additions to dried arrangements, especially since the natural foliage of the flowers has been stripped off before drying. Leaves can be preserved by various methods—silica gel, air drying, pressing—but the most useful is by infusing their veins with a glycerine and water solution. Leaves so treated have a bronzed leathery look and can be immersed in water to accompany fresh flowers as well as to enhance dried arrangements.

Leaves for preserving should be fully grown but not old. Prepare each branch for immersion by crushing a few inches of its woody stem end with a hammer to soften the fibers. Make a solution of hot water and glycerine, available at drugstores. The strength of the solution and the length of the processing depend on the thickness of the leaves to be treated. For example, immerse thick leaves like rhododendron and evergreens in a solution of one part glycerine to two parts water for one to two months. Process medium-weight foliage like boxwood, laurel, beech and holly in a solution of one part glycerine to 2½ parts water for three to four weeks. Immerse thin-leaved branches and vines in a solution of one part glycerine to three parts water for about a week.

Fill a fairly large container with the preserving solution, immerse the branches and leave in a warm dark place—a basement is ideal—for the necessary length of time. Depending on the height and amount of foliage to be treated, useful containers include milk bottles, 1- or 2-pound coffee cans, or tall vases. The glycerine treatment will be completed when the solution has penetrated the veins of the foliage and the leaves are supple and bronze in color. You may need to add additional solution to the container during processing.

If you want to add luster to the treated leaves, spray them with a clear lacquer like Krylon or hair spray. If you want a touch of subtle color, spray a light spattering of soft green paint on a few of the leaves.

STORAGE. Store glycerine-processed leaves in boxes or vases. They need not stand in glycerine solution or water.

FOLIAGE FOR PROCESSING IN GLYCERINE SOLUTION. Foliage from these plants, trees and shrubs can be preserved in glycerine solutions. Plants are listed under their most f........ names:

andromeda
anthurium
bayberry
beech
boxwood
cockscomb (celosia)
dogwood
euonymus
holly
ivy (English)
laurel
lotus
magnolia
maple (Japanese, red, Norway)
oak (white, black, scarlet, scrub)
poplar (white)
rhododendron
rose foliage
sweet gum

DRIED ARRANGEMENTS

Dried arrangements make particularly delightful gifts. They travel beautifully, never wilting en route. They are absolutely care free, requiring no watering or feeding, making them ideal decorative solutions for a busy home or office. They thrive without light or moisture, providing a colorful garden in the very places where nothing will grow. They carry no pollen or perfume, which recommends them highly for sickrooms and allergic friends. And artfully arranged, they are the still lifes of nature, combining form, texture and color in harmonious relationships.

Containers for dried arrangements can be as modest as a straw basket or recycled wine jug or as elaborate as a Royal Crown Derby tureen. Practically any object can be pressed into service to hold a dried arrangement. A host of containers not usually associated with floral bouquets are immediately possible when you no longer need to provide water. Charming arrangements of tiny daisies, baby's breath, and other miniatures are delightfully displayed in an egg coddler, a candlestick, an antique inkwell. Great armfuls of wheat or branches of foliage fill out a ceramic crock, a firewood holder, a brass coal hod. And of course there are pitchers, mustache cups, ginger jars, honey pots, jugs, mugs, tea caddies, miniature chests in all sizes and shapes. Wicker, straw, china, ceramics, pewter, copper—practically any kind of container is appropriate.

Most containers are opaque in order to hide the oasis or florist clay which anchors the flower arrangement; dry sphagnum moss masks the view from above. But if you would like to display your dried wares more openly—perhaps in a Lucite cube, a crystal pitcher, a chemical beaker—partially fill the container with beans, lentils, uncooked macaroni, pretty pebbles, marbles, sand, shells. These will support a handsome display of dried plants.

The arrangements that fill these varied containers should, of course, be appropriate to them. Wild flowers, grasses and pods somehow seem at home in stoneware, straw and other natural settings, just as delicate and sophisticated blossoms cultivated in the flower bed somehow seem wedded to the elegance of china and silver. But be flexible as you mix and match flower to container or you will miss the delightful surprise of arranging your best roses in country pewter or a bunch of strawflowers in a cut crystal creamer.

Moreover, don't be rigid about keeping your woodland and meadow plants separate from your carefully nurtured garden specimens. The most enchanting and interesting arrangements may very well come from a happy marriage of all your dried plants, including as well some glycerine-treated foliage and pressed ferns to bring a welcome touch of bright green.

If your home-dried flowers and leaves don't provide enough stock for all the bouquets and arrangements you want to make, fill in with store-bought botanicals. You may very well need more baby's breath, artemisia, statice and silver dollars, all of which provide excellent background foliage and filler to display colorful dried flowers in mass arrangements. You can buy a wide variety of dried material at florists, dime stores, and by mail.

LUCITE FLORAL DISPLAYS

Embedding dried flowers in plastic is a striking contemporary way to present the products of the drying shed. Encased in clear geometric forms like cubes, pyramids, hemispheres, cylinders or rectangles, single flower heads and three-dimensional compositions make stunning paperweights or decorative ornaments, their colors frozen, their shapes suspended.

Choose forms appropriate to the shapes and sizes of your dried botanicals. A hemisphere, for example, handsomely displays a black-eyed Susan or zinnia; a cube is nicely suited to a globe amaranth, a cylinder to a rosebud or teasel pod. The visual effect is especially dramatic when the plant all but fills the form.

The casting is made with a plastic resin that is mixed with a hardening catalyst. When buying the resin, be sure it is still fresh and use it fairly soon; it has a short shelf life. All necessary supplies are carried in hobby shops.

To make the casting, first measure the capacity of your mold (it may be marked on it). Following the manufacturer's directions, mix only enough resin and catalyst to fill the mold about one-third full. Stir well and pour into the mold; allow the mixture to gel but not harden. At that time, mix the remaining amount of resin and catalyst needed to fill the mold—don't allow for displacement of the embedded plants—and stir well. Pour a small amount of this mixture over the gelled surface and place the flower or plants face down on it; carefully pour the remaining mixture to the top of the mold. Small air bubbles will disappear during the curing; dislodge big bubbles by stirring carefully so as not to disturb the placement of plants. Allow the plastic to set overnight. Release the cured casting by pushing on the reverse side of the mold, like a plastic ice cube tray. Polish the base of the casting smooth with fine sandpaper and buff to a high gloss with rubbing compound. The mold itself is reusable. You can lengthen the life of the mold and insure easy removal of the castings with mold release liquid, available at hobby shops.

PAPERWEIGHT KITS

If you want to display your dried botanicals without embedding them in plastic, you can mount charming small arrangements of dried and pressed materials under the magnifying dome of a paperweight or display a taller arrangement under a glass belljar. This item is widely sold in hobby and craft shops and by mail.

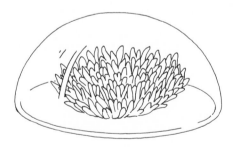

SOURCES OF SUPPLIES

If you cannot find supplies locally or locate them through the classified telephone directory under such listings as Florists, Craft Supplies or Hobby Supplies, here are a few sources for mail order shopping. Some sources have catalogs, for which there is sometimes a charge.

Baskets

The Flower Cart, 3819 North Broadway, Chicago, Ill. 60613
Fran's Basket House, Route 10, Succasunna, N.J. 07876
Holiday Handicrafts, Inc., Winsted, Conn. 06098

Display domes and boxes

Downs, Evanston, Ill. 60204
The Naturalist, P.O. Box 1423, Provo, Utah 84601

Dried botanicals

Roberta Moffitt, 3119 Halesworth Road, Columbus, Ohio 43221
The Naturalist, P.O. Box 1423, Provo, Utah 84601

Paperweight blanks for displaying flowers

Flower Preservations, Inc., Box 301, Golden, Colo. 80401
Holiday Handicrafts, Inc., Winsted, Conn. 06098

Plastic casting supplies for embedments

American Handicrafts, 8112 Highway 80 West, Fort Worth, Texas 76116

Silica gel and other flower preservatives and supplies

Flower Preservations, Inc., Box 301, Golden, Colo. 80401
Roberta Moffitt, 3119 Halesworth Road, Columbus, Ohio 43221

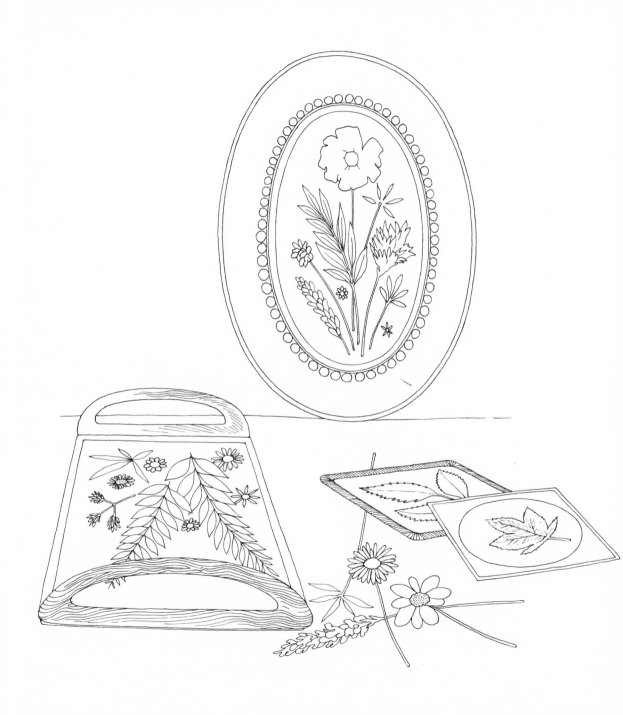

II

PRESSED KEEPSAKES FROM THE GARDEN

Pressed flowers preserve the treasures of the garden in a very special way, delighting the visual sense. Their very flatness, stripped of dimension and scent and sometimes even recognizable color, becomes an intriguing artistic element, transforming a botanical specimen into its abstract representation. Making compositions of these pressed floral forms is a particular pleasure, combining in one creative process the arrangement of botanical shapes and textures with nostalgic recall of the garden and field.

These floral compositions are themselves transformed into handsome keepsakes—framed as pictures, themselves framing small mirrors, wedded to Lucite in coasters, bookends, desk accessories, box covers, trays. They can be sandwiched between plastic sheets as grandly floral placemats or charmingly tipped onto the corners of note paper, invitations, placecards. They can be contemporary or Victorian, handsome or dainty, colorful with blues and yellows or restrained in creamy beige and browns. Their arrangement and style is wherever your garden and fancy lead.

SUITABLE PLANTS FOR PRESSING

The most easily pressed and faithfully rendered flowers are simple and relatively flat, like daisies and pansies. Most leaves and ferns are eminently pressable. Better candidates than the woody sprays of shrubs or trees are the green sprigs of fleshy herbaceous plants and vines, especially trailing varieties whose curving stems will lend grace and motion to your compositions. Also consider gathering the same kind of leaf both in the spring when it is young and green and in the fall for its autumnal color.

You will be intrigued by the final shape and coloration of the pressed bloom which is often quite different from the living blossom. Shape, of course, undergoes interesting transfigurations from full and rounded to flat. Colors, too, undergo their own unpredictable changes. Pink flowers like roses often bleach out to cream or darken to rusty brown; yellows sometimes turn beige or light orange; white flowers usually turn creamy; delphiniums and lobelia hold their blue color but forget-me-nots, campanulas, cornflowers tend to fade. In general, the most reliable colors are yellows, orange, and delphinium blue.

The following plant list is offered as a guide and should not be viewed restrictively. Pick and press everything you see that seems at all possible—ferns, stems, leaves alone and in sprays, large flowers for central focus, small sprigs to fill in background spaces, separate florets and individual petals to reassemble. Your final compositions will benefit from a wide assortment of plant material in as many shades and shapes and sizes as you can amass throughout the growing season.

FLOWERS

acacia	*delphinium*	*pansy*
anthemis	*dogwood*	*phlox*
aster	*freesia*	*poppy*
azalea	*geranium florets*	*primrose*
begonia	*goldenrod*	*Queen Anne's lace*
black-eyed Susan	*heartsease*	*rose*
browallia	*heather*	*saxifrage*
buttercup	*honeysuckle*	*scabiosa*
celandine	*hydrangea*	*statice*
clematis	*impatiens*	*sunflower*
columbine	*Johnny-jump-ups*	*trifolium*
coralbells	*lady's bedstraw*	*trillium*
coreopsis	*larkspur*	*verbena*
cosmos	*lily of the valley*	*wild bleeding heart*
cowslip	*mimosa*	*wildflowers*
crocus	*monkshood*	*wood sorrel*
daisies	*narcissus*	*(oxalis)*

FERNS, GRASSES AND LEAVES

anthurium	*cracaena*	*poplar*
aspen	*croton*	*privet*
ash	*cycas*	*prunus*
barberry	*delphinium*	*raspberry*
beech	*dusty miller*	*rhododendron*
blackberry	*eucalyptus*	*rose*
bramble	*galax*	*rubber plant*
burdock	*geranium*	*rue*
canna	*gladiolus*	*sage*
castor oil plant	*globe thistle (echinops)*	*sassafras*
cat's ear	*honeysuckle*	*senecio*
cattail	*horse chestnut*	*sweet gum*
centaurea gymbocarpa	*ivy*	*sweet pea*
chrysanthemum	*lemon*	*vetch*
cinquefoil	*lotus*	*Virginia creeper*
clematis	*magnolia*	*whitebeam*
clover	*maple*	*wood sorrel*
columbine	*mullein*	*wooly lamb's ear*
coralbells	*oak*	*yucca*
cottonwood	*peony*	

STALKS AND STEMS

anthemis	*clematis*	*primrose*
buttercups	*clover*	

GATHERING AND PRESSING

Pick everything you want to press when it looks its best. For flowers, this will be at the peak of their color, just after the dew has dried. For leaves, it will be when they are well formed but before they are old. Rinse off any dust, remove any damaged or infected leaves or petals.

For optimum results, press as soon as possible after picking lest flowers and leaves wilt. The quickest method is to take your pressing equipment right out to the garden beds or fields with you and press as you go. If you want more time to arrange the blooms or sprays on the drying sheet, carry cut flowers and leaves in a bottle or small pail of water, or wrap their stems in damp moss for the trip home. If necessary, revive limp or wilted leaves and flowers in water before pressing.

The pressing process itself is simple, requiring only some kind of absorbent paper and heavy weights, such as stacks of old magazines, books, bricks or stones to lay on them. You can use facial tissue, sheets of newsprint (the ink on newspapers doesn't seem to affect the plants) or any other kind of absorbent paper, but avoid embossed papers which will leave their imprint on the pressed material. When you go on a flower-gathering expedition any distance from your home, you can use the pages of an old telephone book as a portable press, but transfer the plants to flat papers when you get home because the flexible binding sometimes pushes them out of position and creases them.

If you want more elaborate equipment, you can buy blotting paper and a commercial flower press, but makeshift weights and discarded newsprint are every bit as effective and introduce the happy practice of recycling paper, thus conserving some part of the forest whose leaves and flowers can then be gathered for pressing.

PRESSING TIPS

❀   Lay the plant material carefully on the absorbent sheets because it will dry exactly as placed. Separate leaves on the same stem.

❀   Leave enough room around each flower or petal or leaf to avoid touching or overlapping.

❀   Dry petals and leaves carefully before pressing to reduce their moisture content. If the flowers or plants were damp when picked, and if the weather has been humid, you may have to transfer the plant material to new absorbent paper during the pressing process to prevent mold from developing.

❀   Leaves and petals will press more smoothly and easily if laid face down on the drying paper.

❀   Try to capture the naturally graceful set of the plant, retaining the curve of stems and stalks which later will give line and motion to your pressed flower compositions. If the stem or the plant seems too rigid on the drying sheet, coax it into a more graceful position before pressing.

❀   Try to press each flower with its stem (you can always separate them later), but if it looks stiff and unnatural, or cannot fit on your drying sheet, press its various components individually, separating groups of leaves from the main stem or individual florets from a flower cluster. You can always reassemble the flower later with glue. You can also discard the bumpy center of an otherwise flat flower and replace it in your floral composition with a small flat round flower.

❀ Gather extra stems and stalks to use in compositions, even if they do not have pressable flower heads.

❀ Let stiff stalks wilt a little before pressing so you can bend them into supple and curved lines.

❀ Flatten thick stems and stalks with your thumb or a pencil before pressing.

❀ Press the puffy center of a flower down with your thumb to level it for pressing, then weight it heavily.

❀ Try to press flowers of the same thickness together so they will receive the same pressure.

❀ Press flowers, even those of the same varieties, in different positions—head-on, in profile, askew, at various angles—so you will have a wide range of shapes and forms available for arranging.

❀ Press autumn leaves as soon as their colors change in the fall, well before they dry and fade.

As you finish arranging your botanicals on the pressing sheets, tab each one with the name of the plant material and the date you began pressing it. You might also want to note where you found it. These tabs provide ready identification, reminding you of what you pressed and when it will be dry as well as a ready index system for retrieval when making your compositions.

DRYING

Pile up your sheets of tissues and newsprint, then weight them heavily with books, piles of magazines or bricks. Leave them undisturbed for a month before checking. If any flowers seem particularly damp after

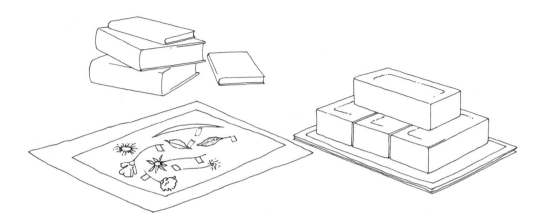

four weeks, or if the absorbent paper they are lying on is still damp, transfer these flowers to clean dry pages or sheets for additional pressing.

Drying time will vary according to the density of the plant material and the dampness of the plants and the weather. Flat thin flowers like lawn daisies will dry thoroughly in a week; other flowers may take up to ten weeks before they are entirely dry. When plants are ready, they will be flat, brittle and fragile. Handle them with care.

STORAGE. You can leave your plants in their press indefinitely, tabbed for future use, since further processing will not hurt them. Or you can store them in boxes in a dry place. For ease of handling you can leave them on their drying sheets with their identifying tabs, or you can layer them between fresh sheets of facial tissues. You may find it helpful to keep the various flowers, ferns, stems, leaves in separate boxes, marking each with its contents. When you want to assemble a floral composition, your plant material will be neatly cataloged; simply lift out the desired sheets of tissue or newsprint and spread out on your work table.

ASSEMBLING A FLORAL COMPOSITION

Assembling a floral composition—called a "florage" by one devoted practitioner—starts from the ground up, that is, with the selection of the background. Traditional grounds are materials like illustration or matte board, and fabrics like velvet, velveteen, denim, wool, burlap, felt, grasscloth and baize in solid colors. Practically any material can be used except slippery fabrics like moire, silk and satin to which the glue may not properly adhere. There is no reason why judiciously chosen designs—pen and ink drawings, wallpaper samples, sheet music, pale checked or striped fabrics—cannot provide interesting backgrounds to floral compositions.

Whatever the color, material or design, the backing must first of all be selected to enhance the pressed flower arrangement. Contrast is essential to set off your plant material, so if your main design uses dark flowers or leaves, choose a light background for greatest contrast. If the primary flowers are light, choose a dark background to set them off. Incidentally, you will find the darker grounds—particularly black, brown and navy—immensely effective. Moreover, since flowers may lose more color after a year or so, dark grounds have the added advantage of compensating for any such future fading, insuring an even stronger contrast between design and background as time goes by.

PREPARING THE BACKING. If your backing material is illustration or matte board, cut it precisely to the finished size with a razor or sharp knife. If you are making a picture, use the glass as a cutting guide. If you are covering an object like a match box or picture frame, take accurate measurements and transfer them to the backing sheet; you may find it helpful to make a template out of heavy cardboard to use as a cutting guide.

If the background is to be decorative paper, it must first be mounted on a sheet of stiff cardboard. You can use illustration or matte board, or any other stiff backing. Glue an ample piece of the paper onto the backing, smoothing out all the wrinkles, then cut it precisely to the finished size you need with a razor or cutting knife. You may even be able to find attractive self-sticking paper such as wallpaper samples.

A fabric background must also first be mounted on a sheet of stiff cardboard. Cut the cardboard just enough smaller than the finished size of the project to allow for the fabric to be turned under at the sides. Then cut a piece of the fabric 1½ inches wider than the cardboard on all four sides, lay it face down on a table, and center the cardboard on it. Cut the four corners of the fabric diagonally to within half an inch of the cardboard, turn in the corners over the cardboard backing, then fold the four sides in over the backing to complete the miter. Put the fabric sides tight enough to make the fabric taut and smooth on the front side yet not so tight as to buckle the cardboard. You can glue the fabric to the back of the cardboard, or tape the fabric flaps down. Do not glue the fabric to the front of the cardboard lest any glue seep through and cause staining.

DESIGNING THE COMPOSITION. Work on a large flat surface with the pressed plant material—flowers, stems, grasses, ferns, leaves—spread out around you. Avoid direct sunlight, which may bleach their color, and breezes and drafts, which may blow them away. If you find any plants the least bit damp, place them in a warm dry place for quick drying. Any dampness incorporated into a composition and sealed into it may eventually cause rot and mildew.

With the prepared backing in front of you, gently move the plant elements around in different arrangements until you get a pleasing design. Use a light touch—a camel's hair paint brush, tweezers, or simply the moistened tip of your finger—to avoid damaging the fragile plants. In general, work from the background, or bottom layer, up, overlapping where desired but always remembering that the finished composition must be flat; its entire top surface will be pressed against a covering glass or plastic sheet, there being no mat to allow even the slightest depth.

While a good design is ultimately a matter of the most personal taste and satisfaction, the following tips may help you get started in what may be a new aesthetic adventure. If you find what seem to be conflicting suggestions, they only emphasize that the creative process is most fun and rewarding when it is flexible and carefree.

❀ For a traditional design center the most colorful and important floral shapes, placing leaves and stems around. Use large and/or darker flowers in the center, smaller and/or lighter flowers toward the edges.

❀ For sweeping lines use long stalks, joining them where necessary and masking the join with an overlapping leaf or petal.

❀ Keep the scale of the flowers and leaves appropriate to the size of the project and arrangement.

❀ Combine the separate parts of different flowers to make new floral forms, for example, placing the flat pressed petals of a black-eyed Susan around a tiny lawn daisy to create your own entirely new "hybrid."

❀ Use individual petals, leaves, flower centers, and stems as simple design elements in their own right, having no relationship to their original floral forms.

❀ Strengthen the color of a particularly pale flower by super-imposing over it another of the same type and color. Or better still, set the top flower a little askew to create interesting shadows and depth as well as increased color intensity.

❀ Superimpose some parts of plants and flowers on others to create the illusion of depth and dimension, eliminating the actual stems and hidden parts of the plant material to keep the composition as flat as possible.

❀ Consider the undersides of leaves as well as their "right" sides; these often have interesting textures and unusual coloring.

❀ Don't overlook the design possibilities of ferns and grasses; they are a wonderful source of motion and definition of line.

❀ Don't crowd your composition. Open space can be an important design element, so leave enough background area for the plants to "breathe."

GLUING THE COMPOSITION. Now that you are completely satisfied with the florage, you are ready to glue it piece by piece to its background. First you must actually clear the background on which you have been making your design. At this point you can make a sketch of your final composition from which to work, or you can turn the whole arrangement out like a cake, the bottom layer coming out on top, which has the added advantage of setting up the layers of the composition in just the order in which they will be glued.

To turn out the composition, lay a sheet of stiff cardboard (any size will do) over the arrangement, hold the "sandwich" tightly together so none of the plant material slips, and turn it upside down. Carefully remove the background sheet now on top and turn it right side up in front of you so you can start gluing the layers of your florage. Remember that although the elements in your composition will be correctly positioned in relation to the whole, they will be the mirror image of your desired arrangement, so be sure to reverse or "flop" each plant element before you glue it.

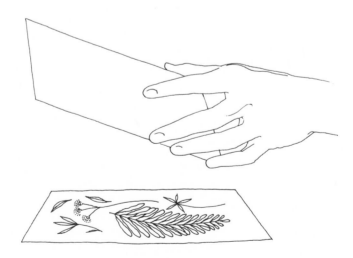

Use water-soluble glue that is white on application and clear when dry, marketed under various commercial names such as Sobo and Elmer's Glue-All. Squeeze a dollop of the glue onto a piece of wax paper and, using a toothpick, dab tiny dots of glue on the back of the plant material. Press the plants into position on the backing, striving for accuracy on the first try; you can move them around easily, but that will leave a stain. Replenish the glue on the wax paper as it gets gummy and hard to use.

Apply the glue sparingly, in part so it doesn't spread beyond the plant and stain the background material and in part to let the plants look "alive." Plants require gluing only at very few basic locations. For instance, a dot of glue at the back of a daisy-like flower will keep the entire head in place. Dab several dots of glue along the length of a multi-leaf spray or a long stem; anchor oval leaves or petals only at their base. These sparse points of contact may appear stingy but they are more than sufficient to secure the florage which, you must remember, will also be held tightly in place by the covering glass or plastic.

After the glue has entirely dried, which will take about an hour, gently clean the backing. If you are framing the florage as a picture, remember to remove dust and fingerprints from both sides of the glass; if you are mounting it in a plastic housing, gently wipe the plastic clean. Then insert the floral composition and, wherever possible, seal the back completely against dust and dampness with tape.

PROTECTIVE PLASTIC SHEETING

You can also protect floral compositions with transparent self-adhesive plastic sheeting sold widely in hardware and dime stores under trade names such as Con-Tact. Cut a piece of the transparent sheeting slightly larger than the backing of your design. Remove its protective paper gradually to expose the adhesive side a little at a time, pressing it over the composition as you go. Work carefully; once applied, the plastic sheet cannot be removed without damaging the flowers and leaves. When the entire surface has been covered, smooth out any remaining wrinkles and cut off the excess plastic with a scissors or razor blade.

As an alternate plastic covering for your composition, you can use a sheet of semi-rigid polyethylene plastic sold in building supply and hardware stores in rolls three feet wide and in various thicknesses. A thickness of five mils is adequate for this purpose. Cut two identical pieces of this plastic with a sharp knife or scissors the same size as your backing sheet, then lay the finished composition between them. Seal the edges together with strips of self-sticking tape. You can use a transparent tape or a plastic-coated cloth tape which is waterproof and available in a range of colors and will provide a frame or border for your design.

This is an easy method for mounting floral pictures, placemats, bookmarks, coasters. Where the project requires, back with self-adhesive felt. The simplicity of the mounting makes this popular for children's projects.

PRESSED FLOWER PICTURES

Framed pictures have always been a traditional and charming way of presenting pressed flower compositions. In pretty gilded oval frames and against a velvet background they evoke nostalgia for the Victorian era. Place them against other backgrounds and they call up different asso-

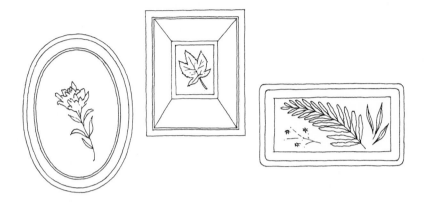

ciations. For example, lay a stark and simple floral composition—perhaps only one perfect bloom and its leaf stem—on a black-and-white line drawing or an architectural rendering. Place a few "tumbled" autumn leaves on a natural linen ground to evoke a drafty November day. Juxtapose the green leaves of a tree, pressed early in the spring growing season, with others from the same tree picked in their glorious autumnal hues and lay your story of evolution on a stylized botanical print.

Whatever your style of presentation, try to make your floral compositions uniquely personal. If you spend a lovely country weekend visiting a friend, gather a few flowers and leaves from her garden for pressing; assemble them when you get home into a pressed floral hostess thank-you. When you travel, pick and press the distinctive flowers, leaves and ferns you find en route and create an unusual souvenir book that will evoke pleasurable memories of your vacation.

Look for ready-made frames of all kinds in craft shops, junk shops and dime stores, and at auctions. You will find an abundance of sizes and shapes—small gilded Italian rounds and ovals; rectangles and squares to spray paint; bamboo frames for an oriental look; dark walnut for a masculine, woodsy appearance.

For a contemporary look, set off your floral compositions in the sparkle of Lucite. Photographic cubes and box frames sold in photographic supply stores make marvelous settings. Other rigid plastic frames and stands are available at art supply stores, museum gift shops, boutiques.

TRAYS

Trays of all kinds are natural showcases for floral compositions. They are particularly easy to custom make, since you can transform practically any picture frame into a tray. Just screw a knob or holder into its short sides.

Perfume trays, fashioned from small frames, are particularly appropriate. Use the pressed petals of perfume-producing flowers—roses, orange blossoms, lavender, violets, lilac—to evoke the bottled scents you keep on the tray.

Larger serving trays can be made from sturdy picture frames. Garden leaves and flowers in handsome arrangement are particularly fitting for serving backyard and terrace guests and make charming gifts for your summer hostesses.

DECORATIVE BOX TOPS

Wooden boxes of all shapes and sizes with recessed tops (originally designed for ceramic tile craft) offer excellent settings for flower compositions. Because there is no covering glass or plastic sheet, protect the florage with transparent self-adhesive plastic sheeting. Place a few drops of glue on the back of the composition and insert into the recess.

Rectangular wooden match boxes provide good surfaces on which to place your pressed flower design. A set of dinner match boxes might each display one perfect bloom and a pair of leaves, a larger kitchen match box would have room for a more elaborate composition, perhaps incorporating the favorite herbs of the cook.

To decorate the top of a match box, first cut the backing board or piece of stiff paper exactly to fit the top surface and glue it to the top of the match box. Design the miniature composition right on the match box and, when finally satisfied with it, glue its components to the backing with tiny dabs of white glue. After the glue has dried, cover the entire composition with a piece of transparent self-adhesive plastic sheeting (see page 54). Trim the excess with a scissors or razor. If desired, decorate the side panels of the match box with tiny floral sprays or strips of fabric or decorative paper.

Clear plastic boxes offer another likely display case. The top of a recipe box, for example, is a charming setting for a design of pressed herb leaves and flowers. Plan it to fit the inside of the lid—facing outward, of course—and protect it against dampness with transparent self-adhesive plastic sheeting (see page 54). Anchor it inside the lid with thin strips of transparent tape concealed at each corner.

LUCITE ACCESSORIES

The clear plastic accessories so popular today—picture frames, coasters, bookends, desk pads, napkin holders—lend a high fashion look to pressed flower compositions. What more dazzling display of an elegant florage than to encase it under the top of a Lucite parsons table? The pressed flower compositions to be inserted in these accessories should be prepared and protected with transparent self-adhesive plastic sheeting as described on page 54.

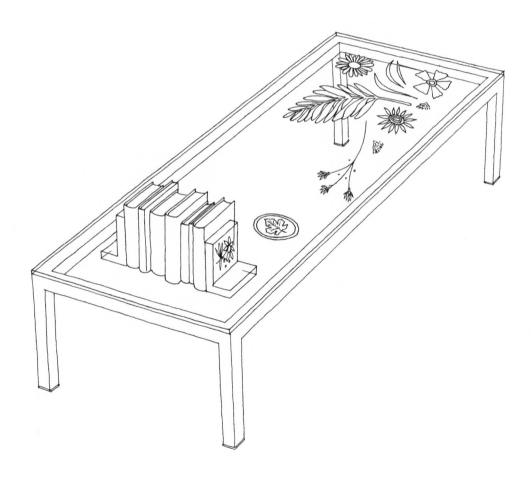

HERBARIUM

If there is a budding botanist of your acquaintance, present an herbarium. This is an album or book of specimens of pressed flowers and other botanicals identified with name, place of collection or origin, and any other classification data of interest. Better yet, present an album with only a few pages of botanicals supplied to indicate the format and the rest of the book blank to encourage the young collector. If you use a looseleaf binder, the specimens can be classified as the collection grows.

Whether you compile a fairly complete collection or present just the album, cover the book with a pressed flower composition. Cut the backing board to exactly the size of the album cover, compose the design, then affix it to the album with a sheet of transparent self-adhesive plastic sheeting turned under on the three free-standing edges. Finish the inside of the cover by masking the turned-under plastic film with a sheet of end paper or decorative self-adhesive sheeting.

NOTE WORTHY

Concern for the permanence of pressed flower craft should not discourage you from creating an array of charming floral presentations that have a shorter life because they cannot be protected by glass or plastic. Note paper, invitations, placecards, greeting cards need no more than a short span of time to convey their messages; they are not kept as permanent keepsakes but enjoyed for their momentary delight. All lend themselves to decoration by small floral and leafy forms. Generally, the plants are placed in a corner or off to one side to preserve as much writing room as possible. Since they will not be held in place by a covering glass, they need to be glued at more locations than other pressed material, perhaps at four or five points.

SOURCES OF SUPPLIES

If you cannot find supplies locally or locate them through the classified telephone directory under such listings as Florists, Craft Supplies, Hobby Supplies, or Picture Frames, here are a few sources for mail order shopping. Some sources have catalogs for which there is sometimes a charge.

Butterflies

The Naturalist, P.O. Box 1423, Provo, Utah 84601

Contemporary picture frames

Kulicke Frames, Inc., 636 Broadway, New York, N.Y. 10012

Lucite accessories

Toni Totes of Vermont, Inc., South Londonderry, Vt. 05155
    (Coasters, bookends, desk organizer, blotter pad, napkin holder, parsons table.)

Plant press

Lilly's Garden, 510 South Fulton Ave., Mount Vernon, N.Y. 10550
The Naturalist, P.O. Box 1423, Provo, Utah 84601

Tray handles

Holiday Handicrafts, Inc., Winsted, Conn. 06098

HERBAL
LOTION

III

AROMATIC VIRTUES

Aromatic virtues recall the fragrance of favored herbs and flowers, teasing our sense of smell with remembrances of gardens past. They come in many shapes and forms—wet, dry, beaded, bagged, potted, packed—but all capture the aroma of the garden, prolonging sweet scents long after the growing season. The perfume of treasured herbs and blooms returns in a potpourri of scented flower chips caught in the glint of a crystal canister; in the elusive aroma emanating from a necklace of rose beads or a linen closet hung with spicy sachets; in the refreshing cool of an herbal lotion. Whatever form they take, aromatics make charming gifts from the garden.

Throughout history, the custom of utilizing the fragrance of flowers and herbs was not merely pleasurable; it had its roots in religious custom and sanitary practices. Aromatic plants were often burned during religious rites, a sweet fragrance to call up the gods, a foul odor to repel evil spirits. In England, church pews were often strewn with herbs and leaves whose scents would be released by the footsteps of parishioners. So beneficial was the fragrance of herbs thought to be that English royalty had a Strewer of Herbs in Ordinary to His Majesty. Homes and public places were strewn with herbs for medicinal purposes, especially during plagues and epidemics. And when people walked through crowded streets, they tried to protect themselves from unseen disease or illness by sniffing bouquets or pomanders hung from waist or neck.

Now that there are more scientific solutions to the prevention and cure of disease, we enjoy aromatics solely for their pleasurable fragrance. So with less abandon than Cleopatra, who liked to sleep on a mattress filled with rose petals, we perfume our homes more subtly with all kinds of potpourris and sweet bags.

POTPOURRIS

Potpourris of fragrant flower petals, dried and cured and combined with aromatic spices and herbs, have been enjoyed from the times of Egyptian kings, when they were a royal luxury, to the Victorian Age when they reached their heyday and became a decorative part of every gentlewoman's home. The earliest potpourris were simply crocks of roses buried in the tombs of the Egyptian kings and left to rot, thus producing the aromas to perfume the royal after-life. By the time of Queen Victoria, other flowers, herbs, spices and oils were added to the traditional rose petals, and the resulting aromatic mix was cured and packed into jars, crocks, porcelains and other decorative containers to perfume the Victorian home.

Today there are both moist and dry potpourris, each using the same ingredients and differing only in their method of preparation. A moist potpourri has a stronger natural scent, sometimes lasting for generations. However, it is not visually attractive because the salt used in the processing bleaches the color from the flower petals, and so it is always packed in opaque jars. A dry potpourri is a visual delight and is often displayed in clear containers so the colors and shapes of the dried flowers will enhance the sense of smell. However, its fragrance relies more on synthetic additives and will last a season or two in an open container, or a year or so if the scent is husbanded.

The following are used in both moist and dry potpourris:

FLOWERS—primarily sweet smelling roses and lavender blossoms and leaves which hold their scent when dried. The most fragrant roses are the old fashioned ones, especially the damask rose, cabbage rose, moss rose and the Provence or French rose. Some hybrids, such as Etoile de Holland, Crimson Glory, Tiffany, Fragrant Cloud, are fragrant enough to use. Check catalogs for fragrance when ordering new rose bushes.

Use both the blossoms and leaves of lavender—true or English lavender, spike lavender, and French lavender.

LEAVES—lemon verbena, fragrant geraniums, mints and other sweet smelling herbs such as basil, rosemary, bee balm, marjoram, lemon balm, sage, woodruff.

SPICES—cinnamon, nutmeg, allspice, ginger, cloves, and seeds of coriander, cardamom, anise; vanilla and tonka beans; angelica.

DRIED CITRUS PEEL—orange, lemon, lime, tangerine.

FIXATIVES. These are the essential addition which helps to blend the various scents into one pleasing fragrance and to insure a lasting aroma. The most common and readily available fixatives are of vegetable origin. They can be purchased in two forms: powdered for moist potpourris, or coarsely ground for dry potpourris:

ORRIS ROOT—a light violet odor from the rhizome of the Florentine iris. Known since ancient times, it is now the most popular fixative.

CALAMUS—a less fragrant violet odor from the rhizome of the sweet flag.

VETIVER—a subtle odor, resembling sandalwood, from a tropical grass. It is often used for sachets because of its reputed moth-retarding qualities.

RESINS—the most popular and easily available is gum benzoin, the fragrant substance from the bark of the spicebush (or Benjamin bush of the Bible).

ANIMAL FIXATIVES have strong, long-lasting odors so must be used sparingly and in combination with other scents. They hold their own and other fragrances a long time:

MUSK—a heavy sweet powerful odor from the male musk deer.

AMBERGRIS—a light pleasant odor like balsam from the sperm whale.

CIVET—a light floral scent.

FRAGRANT OILS. You can purchase oils in wide variety from apothecary shops and perfume suppliers. A few drops added to dried flower petals strengthen and blend the scents and create a longer lasting, more fragrant product.

MOIST POTPOURRI

The Egyptians who left crocks of roses to rot in the tombs of their kings were actually making moist potpourris. In fact, the very word *potpourri* derives from two French words meaning "pot" and "rotted," and accurately describes the moist way of making these aromatic medleys.

The general method for making moist potpourris is to sprinkle layers of partially dried flower petals, mostly roses, with coarse non-iodized salt for curing and, after aging, combine them with fixatives, spices and perfumed oils. Many variations in spices and oils are possible, but here is a general recipe for a classic, long-lasting moist potpourri.

> *6 cups partially dried rose petals*
> *1 cup partially dried lavender blossoms*
> *non-iodized salt*
> *¼ cup dried rosemary*
> *10 dried crumbled bay leaves*
> *2 tablespoons dried orange or lime peel chips*
> *1 tablespoon crushed or powdered allspice*
> *1 tablespoon crushed coriander*
> *1 tablespoon crushed or powdered orris root*
> *1 tablespoon crushed gum benzoin*
> *2 drops each ambergris and bergamot for a citrus accent or*
>   *2 drops heliotrope oil for a sweet accent*

Dry the flower petals a day or two, or just long enough for them to lose about half their moisture and become limp. Pack a wide mouth, straight-sided crock or glass jar—flowers should never come in contact with metal—with the partially dried flowers, alternating half-inch layers of the petals with light layers of salt. Continue layering in this fashion and even if the crock is not full, place a plate or cover over the petals and press down with a heavy weight. It may take several weeks of flower gathering, or even an entire growing season, to accumulate a sufficient amount of petals; simply add layers of petals and salt, weighting the cover after each addition.

After the last batch of petals has been added, leave the crock undisturbed in a cool dark place for about two weeks. Spoon off any excess liquid which may have been extracted, stir with a wooden spoon, and replace the weighted cover for another three weeks of curing.

Remove the cured petals from the crock, shaking any excess salt from the mixture. If the petals are caked together, separate or crumble into small pieces. In a bowl combine the remaining ingredients and stir well. Combine gently but thoroughly with the cured petals. Pack the blended potpourri into opaque containers. Cap tightly and let the mixture ripen and mellow for another two to three weeks.

CONTAINERS. Containers for moist potpourris are always opaque because the salt curing bleaches the color from the flower petals, leaving an unattractive sight but a heavenly smell. Potpourri crocks may be simple pottery jars or elaborate Chinese porcelains or any other decorative ceramic container that strikes your fancy. Traditionally, the jars have two covers: a perforated lid to let the aroma waft into the room, and a cap to close the container completely when its perfumed odors are not desired. If you cannot find a double-lidded container, use a small-necked jar like a ginger jar or recycle a fancy mustard crock. If you want a tiny potpourri jar, recycle a commercial spice or salt-blend dispenser which has a perforated plastic lid. Spray the bottle with paint and decorate with individual floral decals, or swathe the whole jar in a pouf of gaily printed fabric, and secure at the neck with ribbon.

As an added fillip for your potpourri gift, attach an ounce or two of brandy to the potpourri jar, explaining that a moist potpourri can be revived—as who cannot—with an occasional shot of brandy. With such solicitous ministrations, a well-blended moist potpourri will keep its scent for many years.

DRY POTPOURRI

Dry potpourris are meant to be seen as well as sniffed; the pretty shapes and colors of its dried flowers enhance its appearance. Although the actual aroma of a dry potpourri is more delicate than that of a moist one (the drier a flower, the weaker the perfume), what is lost in natural fragrance is made up by supplemental additives and the visual appeal of the pretty buds and petals. Moreover, to the only two flowers that retain their fragrance when dried—roses and lavender—can be added many small colorful buds and petals that retain their good looks and handsome appearance when dried: marigolds, cornflowers, yellow primroses, delphinium, daisies, violets, bachelor's button, pansies, salvia, blue salvia, nasturtium and yarrow, among many others.

Dry potpourris are simpler, neater and cleaner to make than moist ones and so are understandably more popular. The same ingredients are used in both methods, except that for dry potpourris the spices and fixatives must be chopped or crushed rather than powdered, so as not to cloud the glass containers and mask the appearance of the pretty dried petals and buds.

The general method for making a dry potpourri is to combine thoroughly dried petals and leaves with fixatives and blenders, such as spices, rinds and fragrant oils. For best results, pick flowers and leaves in their prime on a dry day, after the dew has dried but well before noon to avoid the hottest sun. Pick only as much as you can dry at one time.

Set up drying racks on an airy porch, in the attic or basement, or other place with gentle ventilation away from the sun. Especially good for this purpose are unused window screens or several thicknesses of newsprint covered with a few layers of cheesecloth to make an absorbent netting.

Remove the petals and fragrant leaves from large or compact

flowers like roses and spread them out in a single layer to dry completely. Discard petals damaged by rain or insects. Small flowers and buds can be dried whole. This drying process will take anywhere from a few days to two weeks.

After the flowers and leaves are chip dry, store them in covered containers until you have accumulated enough for a potpourri. They will keep indefinitely in a cool dry place.

To blend your potpourri according to any of the recipes listed below, gently toss the dried petals and leaves in a big bowl with the fixatives, spices and fruit peel, all crushed in a mortar, and the perfuming oils. If you want to concoct your own blends, use any of the scents listed earlier as potpourri ingredients (pp. 66–68) in the general proportions of one cup of dried petals to one teaspoon of fixative, one teaspoon of spices and a drop or two of perfuming oil.

SWEET ROSE POTPOURRI

2 cups dried rose petals

¼ cup dried lemon verbena

½ cup dried lavender

¼ cup dried sweet woodruff

½ cup dried rose geranium

2 teaspoons crushed cardamom seeds

1 nutmeg, crushed

2 teaspoons crushed tonka beans

5 teaspoons dried orange peel chips

1 tablespoon crushed orris root

4 drops rose geranium oil

2 inch vanilla bean, broken into pieces

CITRUS MINT POTPOURRI

1 cup dried lemon balm

1 cup dried lemon verbena

1 cup dried mint

¼ cup dried lemon peel chips

¼ cup dried lime peel chips

1 teaspoon crushed whole cloves

1 tablespoon crushed orris root

2 drops ambergris

2 drops bergamot oil

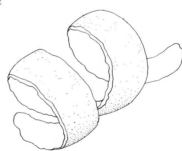

SPICE POTPOURRI

2 cups dried rose petals

2 cups dried lavender

2 tablespoons crushed whole cloves

4 sticks cinnamon, broken

2 nutmegs, crushed

4 tablespoons crushed tonka beans

3 tablespoons crushed cardamom seeds

3 tablespoons crushed coriander seeds

2 tablespoons crushed orris root

2 drops rose geranium oil

6 drops bergamot oil

HERB POTPOURRI

½ cup dried spearmint

½ cup dried lemon balm

½ cup dried thyme

1 cup dried rosemary

½ cup dried sage

½ cup dried summer savory

½ cup dried basil

12 cardamom seeds, crushed

¼ cup dried lemon peel chips

1 tablespoon pulverized benzoin

2 tablespoons crushed orris root

3 drops heliotrope oil

6 drops bergamot oil

Pack the scented mixtures in closed containers to mellow for six to eight weeks, stirring occasionally with a wooden spoon. Until the potpourri has ripened, its scent may seem raw or even vaguely unpleasant. Resist the temptation to add any ingredients until it is fully blended, at which time you can add another drop or two of perfuming oil, if necessary, and age the potpourri further.

When the fragrance has completely mellowed, display the fragrant and colorful petals in sparkling glass containers—old fashioned apothecary jars, contemporary corked cylinders, crystal jam pots. For an especially pretty touch, you can decorate the glass jars with a pressed flower or two, perhaps pansies, violets or even a few leaves. Press them between sheets of newsprint weighted down with a heavy object, then insert them into the crystal container before filling with potpourri and affix them to the inside of the glass with dabs of beaten egg white.

SACHETS

Sachets are nature's air fresheners, small pouches of crushed perfume for scenting clothes, closets, drawers, furniture. They vary in shape, from a flat envelope for layering between the sheets or towels in the linen closet to a plump pouch for hanging in a closet, tucking into an armchair, or inserting into the filling of a decorative pillow.

The dried mixtures of your favorite potpourris can be pulverized to a finer consistency for packing into sachets. This is easily done using a plastic bag and rolling pin. Or you can blend new mixtures for your sachets which incorporate spicier or more astringent scents, and even moth-repelling qualities.

The basic process for making sachets is exactly like that for dried potpourri, except that the resulting dried mixture is finer ground. Traditionally popular were rose petals; the seeds of coriander, anise and caraway; marjoram, basil, rosemary, thyme and lavender; cinnamon, cloves, mace, nutmeg; and such additional scents as lemon and orange peel, vanilla beans, sandalwood and rosewood. These mixtures would incorporate any of the traditional fixatives—musk, civet, ambergris, orris root, and benzoin. Any combination and proportion of herbs was appropriate, used in the general proportions of one quart of herbs and flowers, finely crushed, to 2 tablespoons of spices and 2 tablespoons of fixative.

CLASSIC VICTORIAN SACHET

⅓ cup finely crushed dried verbena
1 cup finely crushed dried lavender
⅓ cup finely crushed dried rose geranium
1 tablespoon crushed orris root

SPICY SACHET

2 *cups finely crushed dried rose petals*
½ *cup finely crushed dried lavender*
½ *cup finely crushed dried rose geranium*
1 *tablespoon crushed whole cloves*
3 *tablespoons dried orange peel chips*
1 *tablespoon crushed coriander*
2 *tablespoons crushed orris root*
4 *drops ambergris*

To the fresh scent of outdoors that sachets bring to clothes and closets can be added moth repellent qualities which are found in particular plants such as wormwood, southernwood, bay laurel leaves and vetiver root. These moth repellent fragrances can be blended with different dominant scents.

I

½ *cup finely crushed dried pennyroyal*
½ *cup finely crushed dried rosemary*
½ *cup finely crushed dried wormwood*
2 *tablespoons dried lemon peel chips*
1 *tablespoon crushed cloves*
1 *tablespoon crushed orris root*
2 *tablespoons crushed vetiver root*

II

½ *cup finely crushed dried mint*

½ *cup finely crushed dried thyme*

½ *cup finely crushed dried southernwood*

2 *tablespoons dried orange peel chips*

1 *tablespoon finely crushed allspice*

1 *tablespoon crushed orris root*

2 *tablespoons crushed vetiver root*

III

½ *cup finely crushed dried lavender*

½ *cup finely crushed dried tansy*

½ *cup finely crushed dried southernwood*

1 *teaspoon crushed orris root*

2 *tablespoons crushed vetiver root*

IV

⅓ *cup finely crushed dried lavender*

⅓ *cup finely crushed dried mint*

⅓ *cup finely crushed dried rosemary*

4 *tablespoons crushed vetiver root*

SACHET BAGS. Pack your sachet mixtures in gaily printed fabric bags of beguiling shapes. The fabric should be tightly enough woven to prevent the dry perfume from trickling out but not so thick or dense as to bury the delicate aromas. Fabrics particularly suitable for sachet bags include organdy, sprigged muslin, handkerchief linen, checked gingham, voile, batiste, dimity. Choose fabrics and trimmings that are festive and charming in themselves, then coordinate them to the scent you are enclosing, using green, gold, mauve, pink and other colors suggestive of the scent and flowers that make up your sachet.

The simplest sachet bag is made from a pretty handkerchief. Almost as easy to use is a 4- to 5-inch square or circle of a suitable fabric; pink the edges or make a neatly rolled hem for a finer finish. Place a tablespoon or two of the dried sachet mixture in the center of the handkerchief or fabric, draw the edges up around the mixture to make a pouf shape, and secure with a rubber band. Conceal the elastic with a ribbon or length of yarn in a pretty color or print, and tie on a sprig of identifying herb.

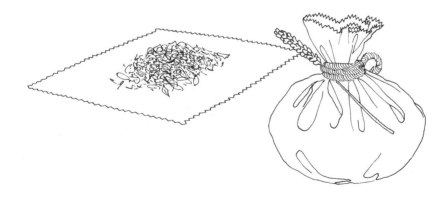

Other shapes also make delightful sachets. Stitch up a small flat envelope for your linen closet or to tuck into a decorative pillow. If you do needlepoint, make up a fragrant mini-pillow with a flower to identify your sachet scent or an aromatic pin cushion for a friend who plies a needle—embroidery, sewing, needlepoint or otherwise. Consider a checked butterfly to hang in a closet, a bright red ball to lend a spicy scent to the Christmas tree, a small Raggedy Ann doll to prop up on a young friend's window sill, a simple tulip to plant among the under-clothes.

From simple square to flower form, any of these shapes are easily made. Cut two identical pieces of material in the shape you want—rectangle, tulip, butterfly, bell, doll. Baste the two pieces of fabric right sides together, leaving a small opening an inch or two wide at the top. Machine stitch over the basting line. Through the opening you have left turn the form right side out and fill with your sachet mixture. If you want to plump out the stuffing, pack small pieces of fiberfill into the corners. Blind stitch the opening, adding a yarn or ribbon tie for a hanging sachet.

BATH SACHETS

A luxurious soak in a hot tub is a pleasure that has been enjoyed since the thermal baths of ancient Egypt and Greece. The ancient Romans perfected the sociability of public bathing and enjoyed the therapeutic effects of herbal baths. Thyme, lavender and rosemary were used, regarded as tonics for tired muscles and other ailments, and as energizing bracers. Today, while commercial bath salts and bath oils clamor for attention, the simple garden-fresh sachet can impart its re-freshing fragrance to the toilette.

Many garden variety herbs can lend their aromatic presence to the bath. Try any of the following for a bath fragrance: lavender, sage, rosemary, pennyroyal, camomile, thyme, any of the mints, and a mint-thyme medley. Traditionally, these herbs were steeped in boiling water and the resulting infusion strained and poured into the tub, but the easiest way to enjoy an herbal bath is with a sachet bag that can be tied to the faucet so the hot water passes through it as the bath is drawn. The bag itself can be dropped into the full tub to steep while the bath is taken.

To make a bath sachet, fill a 4-inch square of cheesecloth or a simple handkerchief with a quarter cup of whole dried herbs. Gather the square in a pouf and tie with a dainty ribbon of appropriate color— mint green, lavender, citrus yellow, rose pink—and leave a tail of ribbon long enough to tie the bath fragrance onto the faucet. Pack a bather's dozen in a pretty flowered shower cap or a shiny glass apothecary jar that can be recycled with bath salts, or mound a few sachets in a scallop shell that can later house bath soap.

AROMATIC FRESHENERS

Happy companions to bath sachets are herbal rubbing lotions, those aromatic fresheners made by steeping a medley of herbs in alcohol. To one cup of fresh lavender leaves add ¼ cup of fresh lemon verbena leaves or ¼ cup each fresh mint leaves and rosemary sprigs. Place the mixture in a clean glass jar and press down with a wooden spoon. Add two cups of unscented rubbing alcohol, cover, and let the mixture steep two to three weeks. Strain the liquid through two layers of cheesecloth into pretty bottles. Cap tightly and label, noting prominently on the label the lotion is not to be used internally. Tie a lavender or green ribbon around the neck of the bottle. Or pair with a lavender or mint bath sachet.

ROSE BEADS

The last rose of summer may become autumn's fashion fancy in the form of an aromatic necklace. Fragrant rose beads, artifacts from colonial days, are made by chopping, cooking, drying and shaping rose petals to form black beads. Worn next to the skin, they give off a light and pleasing odor.

For thirty rose beads the size of marbles, or sixty smaller ones, you will need 4 cups of sweet-smelling rose petals cut fine with a scissors. The petals should be fresh and clean. Place them in a cast iron pot or skillet, barely cover them with water (about one cup), and add a dozen rusty nails to oxidize and blacken the rose petals. Simmer the mixture slowly about an hour, then remove from the heat. Stir with a wooden spoon and leave overnight. Repeat the process several more days until the rose mixture darkens, adding water when necessary to prevent burning and to reach a dark pulpy consistency.

When the rose pulp is sufficiently dark, set the mixture aside for a few days until dry enough to handle. Form the petals into beads by rolling bits of the rose pulp into balls. Make the balls slightly larger than the desired size since some shrinkage will take place during drying.

Lay the beads on several layers of paper toweling for 24 to 48 hours, or until they are partially dry and can be handled. Thread a needle with dental floss, then pierce a hole through the center of each bead and string them at well-spaced intervals.

To complete the drying process, suspend the strand of beads so that air can circulate freely. Rotate the beads occasionally to keep the holes open. Complete drying will take a few days to about a week.

String the beads in combination with coffee beans, polished shells and stones, nuggets of oiled woods, pieces of coconut shell, cork stoppers, beads of other colors, even semi-precious stones, transforming these natural treasures into intriguing fashion accessories.

CATNIP PADS

The mint family, whose abundant varieties produce soothing teas, zesty jellies, and refreshing aromatics, offers a beguiling gift for cats as well. The mint with an extraordinary attraction for cats is catnip. Appropriately known also as cat-mint, its aroma sends felines into frenzies of playful excitement.

If there is a feline on your gift list, a sturdily constructed pillow or toy containing a small bag of this dried herb will be the cat's miaow. Hang small bunches of the gray-green heart-shaped leaves to dry for about a week in a well-ventilated area. Then fill a small cheesecloth bag with dried, crumbled leaves and tuck it into a ready-made pillow by slitting open just enough seam to insert the bag, then blind stitch the opening together.

You can also make your own small catnip pillow or pad. Take two identical pieces of calico and sew them, leaving a small opening on one of the sides. Through this opening insert the bag of catnip, plump out the pad by stuffing with cotton, and blind stitch the opening. For a really gala gift, make a mouse-shaped toy of gray flannel and stuff with catnip. Add a gray yarn tail and you'll see the best cat-and-mouse game in town.

PLANTS TO GROW FOR AROMATIC VIRTUES

basil	*lemon verbena*	*southernwood*
bee balm (bergamot)	*marjoram*	*summer savory*
camomile	*mints*	*tansy*
catnip	*pennyroyal*	*thyme*
geraniums, fragrant	*rosemary*	*woodruff*
lavender	*roses*	*wormwood*
lemon balm	*sage*	

SOURCES OF SUPPLIES

If you cannot find supplies locally or locate them through the classified telephone directory under such listings as Florists, Nurserymen, Pharmacists, Herbs, Perfumes, or Oils—Essential, here are a few sources for mail order shopping. Some sources have catalogs for which there is sometimes a charge.

Herb stock

Caprilands Herb Farm, North Coventry, Conn. 06238
Cook's Geranium Nursery, 712 North Grand, Lyons, Kan. 67554
Hemlock Hill Herb Farm, Litchfield, Conn. 06759
Hilltop Herb Farm, Box 866, Cleveland, Texas 77327
Shirley Morgan, 2042 Encinal Ave., Alameda, Calif. 94501
Nichols Garden Nursery, 1190 Pacific Highway, Albany, Ore. 97321
Pine Hills Herb Farm, Box 307, Roswell, Ga. 30073
Sunnybrook Farms Nursery, 9448 Mayfield Road, Chesterland, Ohio 44026

Labels for jars and bottles

The Herb Farm Country Store, 380 North Granby Rd., Route 189, North Granby, Conn. 06060

Potpourri jars and porcelain pomander balls

Caswell-Massey Co., Ltd., 320 W. 13 St., New York, N.Y. 10014
The Country Gourmet, 512 South Fulton Ave., Mt. Vernon, N.Y. 10550
The Herb Cottage, Washington Cathedral, Mount St. Alban, Washington, D.C. 20016

Potpourri supplies, oils, fixatives

Aphrodisia, 28 Carmine St., New York, N.Y. 10014

Caprilands Herb Farm, North Coventry, Conn. 06238

Caswell-Massey Co., Ltd., 320 W. 13 St., New York, N.Y. 10014

Fioretti, 1472 Lexington Ave., New York, N.Y. 10028

Haussman's Pharmacy, 6th and Girard Ave., Philadelphia, Pa. 19123

The Herb Cottage, Washington Cathedral, Mount St. Alban, Washington, D.C. 20016

The Herb Farm Country Store, 380 North Granby Rd., Route 189, North Granby, Conn. 06060

Herb Products Co., 11012 Magnolia Blvd., North Hollywood, Calif. 91601

Hilltop Herb Farm, Box 866, Cleveland, Texas 77327

Indiana Botanic Gardens, Inc., P.O. Box 5, Hammond, Ind. 46325

Kiehl Pharmacy, Inc., 109 Third Ave., New York, N.Y. 10003

Nature's Herb Co., 281 Ellis St., San Francisco, Calif. 94102

Roses

Joseph J. Kern Rose Nursery, Box 33, Mentor, Ohio 44060

Will Tillotson's Roses, Brown's Valley Road, Watsonville, Calif. 95076

IV

CULINARY DELIGHTS

Gifts for the kitchen spring with obvious abundance from the herb garden whose culinary treasures can be transformed into a plentitude of delights: crocks of fresh salted herbs, jars of dried leaves, aromatic tea blends, *bouquets garnis*, herb butters, vinegars, salts, mustards, sugars and jellies. Harvesting an edible crop from the flower bed is at least as rewarding, perhaps because it is less expected. As King Charlemagne observed, "Flowers are the friend of physicians and the praise of cooks." A variety of flowers can come to the dining table in various guises—candied, crystallized, jellied, pickled—to accompany the more familiar freshly blooming centerpiece.

A cautionary note: When you are planning to dazzle a friend with a culinary delight from the flower bed, don't substitute your favorite bloom for one specified in a recipe, and don't experiment with alternate species. Some flowers are not edible at all, some must be cooked before eating, others are poisonous in any form. And as with all fresh plant material, use only those herbs and flowers that are free from disease and that have been sprayed, if at all, with a non-toxic, water-soluble spray or insecticide which can be rinsed off completely.

Some of these culinary delights may be new to your friends. They will appreciate a note suggesting ways to enjoy your gifts from the garden.

CANDIED FLOWERS AND LEAVES

One of the prettiest ways of preserving the appearance, taste, and sometimes even the aroma of favorite leaves and flowers is to candy or crystallize them. Perfectly formed leaves and just-opened blossoms with a snowy dusting of sugar make enchanting decorations for cakes, puddings, sherbets and other desserts. Although they take care and patience to make, they are especially valued gifts.

Best suited to candying are violets, rose petals, lilac florets, orange blossoms, blue star-shaped borage blossoms and mint leaves. Pick and use them when they are at the peak of their form and freshness.

> *leaves or flowers (see above)*
> *florist wire, toothpicks, paper towels, Styrofoam blocks*
> *3 tablespoons gum acacia powder*
> *1 cup water*
> *1 cup granulated sugar*
> *food coloring to match the color of flowers or leaves (optional)*
> *superfine sugar*

Rinse about 20 leaves or flowers with a fine misting of cool water. Separate the leaves and flowers from all but ¼ inch of the stem and affix each leaf or flower to a 3-inch piece of florist wire. Let the plants dry thoroughly on paper towels.

In the top of a double boiler heat the gum acacia powder (available from drug stores) with ½ cup of water, stirring until the mixture is thoroughly dissolved. Let cool to room temperature.

Dip each flower or leaf, one at a time, in the cooled solution, holding it by its wire "stem." Coat all sides of the plant well and set aside to dry for about two hours; use toothpick to separate petals so flowers dry in a pretty shape. Stick the wires into a piece of Styrofoam so the flowers can drain and dry completely.

Prepare the candying syrup in a heavy saucepan. Combine 1 cup granulated sugar in ½ cup of water and stir until the mixture comes to a boil. Then insert a candy thermometer and let the syrup cook without stirring until the temperature reaches 238° F. or soft ball stage. If desired, add a few drops of food coloring to brighten the appearance of the flowers or leaves. Set the syrup aside to cool.

Dip each well-dried flower or leaf, one at a time, in the cooled syrup, holding it by its wire stem until all surfaces are well coated. Drain excess, dip gently in superfine sugar. You can sugar each leaf or flower thoroughly or dust it lightly so some color still shows through. Set the candied plants on their wire stems into a Styrofoam block to dry thoroughly, for eight hours or overnight. Remove wires, then pack plants gently in airtight containers between sheets of wax paper.

FLAVORED SUGARS

Rose petals, lemon balm, lemon verbena, fragrant geranium leaves and fragrant mints all lend their distinctive flavors to sugars which will in turn enhance the taste of fruit salads, teas, punch bowls, icings and baked desserts.

> ¼ *cup fresh leaves*
> 1 *cup superfine sugar*

Wash and dry the leaves carefully. In a storage container alternate layers of sugar and leaves so that the leaves are evenly distributed. Cap the container tightly and leave for two to three weeks.

Strain out the dry leaves. Pack the flavored sugar in a tightly stoppered glass container. For decoration and identification, place a freshly pressed leaf or sprig of the herb against the inside of the glass jar before filling. Always welcome are suggested uses for the various sugars: sugar-minted iced tea, lemon verbena sprinkled over summer strawberries, a rose geranium icing, a dusting of rose petal sugar over pound cake or plain cookies, a holiday punch sweetened with lemon balm sugar and decorated with pretty sprigs of the herb.

HOREHOUND CANDY

Horehound is an old world herb of the mint family whose medicinal qualities have been used since ancient times to relieve sore throats and coughs; it probably was used to make the world's first cough syrup, but since the 19th century, it has been used to flavor hard candy, which is more like sweetened cough drops. Horehound drops may not be everyone's piece of candy, but they do have a long and honorable tradition.

¼ cup dried crushed horehound leaves
2 cups boiling water
2½ cups granulated sugar
½ cup light corn syrup
6 drops oil of peppermint
10 drops green food coloring
1 cup superfine sugar

Oil a jelly roll pan, about 15 by 10 inches. Steep the horehound leaves in boiling water for 15 minutes. Strain into a large heavy saucepan. Add granulated sugar, corn syrup and cook over medium heat, stirring until the sugar is dissolved and the mixture comes to a boil. Insert a candy thermometer and cook without stirring until the temperature reaches 300° F., or hard crack stage. Remove mixture from heat and stir in oil of peppermint and food coloring. Pour into prepared pan and score into inch-square pieces before candy sets.

After candy has set, break into pieces, roll in sugar and pack between layers of wax paper in an airtight container. Makes about 1½ pounds.

APPLEMINT DROPS

1 cup applemint or peppermint leaves
1½ cups apple juice
2 cups sugar
2 to 3 drops of green food coloring
¼ teaspoon cream of tartar

Oil a cookie sheet or miniature muffin tins.
Place the mint leaves and apple juice in a stainless steel or enamel

saucepan. Bring to a boil, cover, and remove from heat. Let steep 15 minutes.

Strain through several layers of cheesecloth into a 3-quart saucepan. Add sugar and cook over medium heat, stirring until the sugar is dissolved and mixture comes to a boil. Insert candy thermometer and cook without stirring until temperature reaches 240° F., or soft ball stage. Remove from heat and add food coloring. Beat in cream of tartar and continue to beat until mixture becomes creamy. Immediately drop by teaspoonfuls on prepared cookie sheet, miniature muffin tins, or into paper candy cups. Makes about 1 pound.

MAY WINE

May wine is a delightful springtime tradition from Germany. The essential ingredient is woodruff, a decorative herb with shiny leaves and tiny white blossoms, which grows well in a shady corner of the herb garden. To magically transform white wine into May wine, simply place several sprigs of woodruff in a bottle of Rhine or Moselle, replace the stopper and allow the flavor to ripen for a day or two.

Accompany a gift of May wine with a bunch of fresh woodruff and directions for preparing the May Bowl, a refreshing punch invoking a springtime garden.

MAY BOWL

½ *gallon May wine*
1 *cup sliced strawberries*
½ *cup superfine sugar*
1 *orange, thinly sliced*
1 *lemon, thinly sliced*
1 *bottle champagne*

Place ingredients over a large block of ice in a punch bowl. Decorate with sprigs of the woodruff.

DANDELION WINE

Recycling any outworn object to another use is always a pleasurable operation, but transforming an unwanted weed into both a tender salad and a fruity wine is surely a heady accomplishment. Dandelions, those unwelcome intruders in a well-tended lawn, present the opportunity. Pick young dandelions from lawns or open fields early in the season before the serrated leaves—those *dents de lion* or lion's teeth that give the plant its name—grow tough and the bright yellow flowers have gone to seed. Use the young green leaves in a fresh garden salad, and collect sufficient dandelion petals to make a wine. To gather the petals, hold the plant by the stem and calyx and twist the flower head off. Wash the flower heads carefully to remove any traces of spray, fertilizer, or other chemical treatment.

4 cups dandelion petals

2 quarts water

1 orange, thinly sliced

1 lemon, thinly sliced

3 cups sugar

6 whole cloves

2 cinnamon sticks

1-inch piece of ginger root

½ package dried yeast

¼ cup warm water

3 sterile pint bottles

Place washed petals in a crock. Boil the water and pour over the petals. Let them steep in the crock at room temperature for one week.

Put the orange and lemon slices and sugar in a large stainless steel or enamel saucepan and press the fruit with a wooden spoon. Strain the steeped dandelion liquid into the saucepan, discarding the petals, and add the cloves, cinnamon sticks and ginger root. Bring the mixture to a boil, stirring carefully, and let simmer half an hour. Cool to lukewarm.

While the brew is cooling, completely dissolve the yeast in the warm water, then add to the saucepan. Let the liquid stand uncovered at room temperature for two days.

Strain the brew through filter paper into a crock or large glass jar. Cover and let stand for three weeks.

Strain wine into sterile bottles, cork, and store three to six months in a cool place before using.

Makes 3 pints.

DILLY BUDS

While each bloom of the day lily only lasts a day, the edible buds can be picked and savored for months. And even though each flower blooms and withers so quickly, the supply of buds is plentiful; each day lily plant has up to a dozen or more flower stems, and each stem may carry up to fifty buds. Day lilies bloom abundantly along roadsides as well and are much used in flower cookery. Here is a delightful recipe for pickled buds to give—and serve—as an exotic addition to the relish tray.

> 4 *cups day lily buds*
> 4 *sterile half pint jars*
> 2 *teaspoons dill seeds*
> 2 *teaspoons mustard seeds*
> 2 *teaspoons celery seeds*
> 4 *shallots*
> 1½ *cups herb vinegar*
> ½ *cup water*
> 1 *teaspoon salt*

Wash day lily buds carefully and drain. Drop washed buds into a pot of boiling water and boil for one minute. Drain, and pack buds into

4 sterile half-pint jars. Distribute the dill seeds, mustard seeds, celery seeds and shallots evenly among the jars.

Place the herb vinegar, water and salt in an enamel or stainless steel saucepan and bring to a boil. Pour the mixture over the buds to within half an inch of the top of the jars. Seal and refrigerate.

NASTURTIUM CAPERS

Nasturtium is a flower that ought to be grown as much for its culinary as its ornamental value, for every part of the plant has long been known to cooks. Even its name, translated from the Latin, literally means nose twister, referring, according to Pliny, to its pungent bite and scent. The round leaves are peppery, somewhat like watercress to which the plant is related, and make a spicy and delicious salad green. The bright red, orange and yellow flowers were thought to have healing qualities, and perhaps because of their sharp flavor, were served on bread and butter to sharpen the wits; the plant does indeed contain vitamin C and was thought to cure scurvy. The seeds were sometimes ground for a mustard or, as in the following recipe, pickled and used as a subsitute for capers in sauces or meat and fish salads. Pick the young green seeds right after the blossoms drop and before the seeds dry out.

12 *tablespoons salt*
2 *quarts water*
1 *cup nasturtium seeds*
4 *sterile 2-ounce jars*
½ *teaspoon mustard seed*
½ *teaspoon dill seed*
1 *cup cider vinegar*
1 *teaspoon salt*
1 *teaspoon peppercorns*
1 *clove garlic, quartered*

In a glass or ceramic pot dissolve 6 tablespoons of salt in a quart of water. Add the nasturtium seeds and let them soak overnight.

Drain the seeds and repeat the process with fresh water and salt.

Drain, then divide the seeds into four small sterile jars, about 2-ounce capacity. Divide the mustard and dill seeds equally into the four jars.

Into a stainless steel or enamel pot bring the vinegar to a boil with 1 teaspoon salt, peppercorns and garlic. Strain the liquid and pour into the jars over the seeds. Cap the jars tightly and refrigerate.

SHARP HERB MUSTARD

Here is an unusual condiment for boiled beef and other simply prepared meats and cheese. It depends for its herbal tang on dried rather than fresh herbs.

½ *cup powdered mustard*
2 *teaspoons finely crushed dried rosemary*
2 *teaspoons finely crushed dried thyme*
1 *teaspoon salt*
½ *teaspoon sugar*
½ *teaspoon garlic powder*
3 *tablespoons sauterne*
2 *tablespoons herb vinegar*
2 *tablespoons oil*

In a small bowl place the mustard, rosemary, thyme, salt, sugar and garlic powder. Combine the sauterne, vinegar and oil and gradually beat into dry ingredients with a whisk. Store in a covered jar in the refrigerator.

VINEGARS

Herb and flower vinegars make enchanting gifts. They are easy to brew and bottle and are one of the best ways of preserving the culinary wonders of the garden. Consider as a gift a pair of vinegars—one a familiar herb blend, the other an exotic and perhaps less familiar flower brew: a tarragon or basil vinegar for marinating vegetables paired with a carnation vinegar with which to dress a fruit salad; a mint vinegar to spice a lamb roast accompanying a nasturtium vinegar for a tossed green salad. Bottle them in tightly stoppered carafes, apothecary jars, decanters, or even recycled wine bottles and add a fresh leaf or petal of the bottled flavor for decoration and identification.

HERB VINEGARS. Alone or in combination, the following herbs are most suitable for flavoring vinegars: basil, tarragon, dill, mint, summer savory, thyme and lemon balm. The best vinegars to use are cider, red wine or white wine vinegar. One cup of fresh herb leaves or sprigs, or ½ cup dried herbs, nicely flavors one quart of vinegar. Here are general directions:

Pick young leafy sprigs just before the plant flowers. Wash and dry them carefully, discarding any woody stems. Put the leaves, fresh or dried, in a large clean jar and crush slightly with a wooden spoon.

In a stainless steel or enamel saucepan heat the vinegar to just under boiling. Pour over the herbs and cap the jar tightly with a non-rusting lid; if your jar has a metal cap, place a small piece of foil over the jar before capping. Let steep two to three weeks.

Strain the vinegar through cheesecloth into tightly stoppered gift containers. Insert a large fresh leaf or sprig of the herb into each jar before closing and, as before, be certain the vinegar does not come in contact with any metal surface that might rust. Store at room temperature.

MIXED HERB VINEGARS offer an opportunity for an especially distinctive gift from your garden. Here are two happy combinations:

SUMMER SAVORY AND BASIL VINEGAR

½ *cup summer savory leaves or* ¼ *cup dried crumbled leaves*
½ *cup basil leaves or* ¼ *cup dried crumbled leaves*
4 *cloves garlic*
1 *quart red wine vinegar*

Crush the two herbs and the garlic cloves slightly in a clean jar, steep the vinegar, and follow directions above.

TARRAGON AND LEMON BALM VINEGAR

½ *cup tarragon sprigs or* ¼ *cup dried crumbled leaves*
½ *cup lemon balm leaves or* ¼ *cup dried crumbled leaves*
4 *shallots*
1 *quart white wine vinegar*

Crush the two herbs and shallots slightly in a clean jar, steep the vinegar, and follow directions above.

Accompany your gift of vinegars with a favorite recipe, perhaps a marinade or a special salad dressing. Here is a vinaigrette sauce with multidinous uses—as a marinade for meat or cold vegetables or to dress up a tossed green salad. This simple recipe can be written on a string tag and tied right to the neck of the vinegar bottle.

VINAIGRETTE SAUCE

2 cups oil
½ cup herb vinegar
1 tablespoon Dijon mustard
1 tablespoon salt
2 cloves garlic, chopped
1 tablespoon capers

Combine all ingredients in a tightly capped jar and shake well before using.

FLOWER VINEGARS. For most people, these vinegars are an edible bonus from the flower beds, which are more customarily enjoyed for their showy blooms than for their culinary assets. They are made the same way as herb vinegars, except that the flower petals rather than the leaves are steeped, and the vinegar is heated only to lukewarm.

CARNATION VINEGAR

Known in Elizabethan times as the gillyflower or clove pink, carnations have a sweet clove-like aroma and taste. They were once added to beer and wine for spicy flavoring, now make a delightful vinegar with which to dress a summer fruit salad.

1 cup carnation petals
4 cups white wine vinegar
6 cloves

Pull the petals off the flower stems; snip and discard white heels. Wash carefully and dry well. Heat the vinegar to lukewarm.

Place the flower petals and cloves in a clean jar and crush gently with a wooden spoon. Cover with the warm vinegar and cap tightly. If the cap is metal, cover first with a piece of foil. Let the mixture steep about three weeks, preferably on a sunny windowsill.

Strain the vinegar through cheesecloth into decorative bottles and cap or cork tightly.

ELDER FLOWER VINEGAR

Elder flowers are white and sweet tasting, often used for wine making. The vinegar happily complements a pear or Waldorf salad. Gather the elder flowers in early summer.

> 1 *cup elder flowers*
> 4 *cups white wine vinegar*
> ½ *teaspoon sugar*
> 2 *tablespoons whole allspice*

Pull the petals off the stem and wash and dry them carefully. Heat the vinegar to lukewarm.

Place flower petals, sugar and allspice in a jar and crush gently with a wooden spoon. Cover with the warm vinegar and cap tightly. If the cap is metal, cover first with a piece of foil. Let the mixture steep about three weeks, preferably on a sunny windowsill.

Strain the vinegar through cheesecloth into decorative bottles, and cap or cork tightly.

NASTURTIUM VINEGAR

One folktale from Peru has an Indian carrying a sack of gold down a mountainside during the great 16th-century Peruvian gold rush. As he was overtaken by treasure hunters, he implored the gods to take back their gold. Struggling with the intruders, his sack fell open and where the gold nuggets fell there sprang up golden nasturtiums. The leaves and blossoms of this golden bounty add zest to many dishes—salads, sauces, fish and meat alike. Their tangy taste can be captured in a flavorful vinegar.

> 1 *cup nasturtium petals*
> 4 *cups red wine vinegar*
> ¼ *cup dill sprigs*
> 2 *shallots*
> 6 *peppercorns*

Pull the petals off the stem, and wash and dry them carefully. Heat the vinegar to lukewarm.

In a clean jar place the flower petals, dill, shallots and peppercorns and crush gently with a wooden spoon. Cover with the warm vinegar and cap tightly. If the cap is metal, cover first with a piece of foil. Let the mixture steep about three weeks, preferably on a sunny windowsill.

Strain the vinegar through cheesecloth into clean decorative bottles, and cap or cork tightly.

BASIL PESTO

Absolutely nothing recalls the freshness and aroma of a summer herb garden more pungently than a bowl of pesto, that wonderfully aromatic basil concoction to spoon over spaghetti. It freezes beautifully in a pretty glass apothecary jar, offering the taste of summer any time of the year.

> 2 *cups firmly packed torn basil leaves*
> ½ *cup parsley sprigs*
> ½ *cup oil*
> 1 *or 2 cloves garlic*
> 3 *tablespoons pignoli nuts or chopped walnuts*
> 1 *teaspoon salt*

Put all the ingredients in a blender jar and process at medium speed until the mixture is a thick puree. Use a rubber spatula to scrape the sides occasionally and push all the ingredients down into the blades. Spoon into a jar and pour a thin film of oil over to prevent discoloring. Cap tightly.

When ready to serve, warm the pesto gently, toss it with a pound of well drained spaghetti, and serve with grated parmesan cheese.

HERB BUTTERS

Fresh herbs happily make the trip from garden to table in the company of butter, blended and flavored to enhance many dishes. Fresh herbs, of course, retain their flavor best, but some of your dried herbs can easily be combined with fresh herbs into delectable flavored butters. They make especially charming gifts, packed prettily in apothecary jars, stoneware crocks, or any capped container. They keep well up to a week in the refrigerator or can be frozen for future use or gift giving. Here are two of our favorites:

HERB BUTTER I
1 *cup butter, softened*
2 *teaspoons lemon juice*
4 *tablespoons minced fresh tarragon leaves or 2 tablespoons*
   finely crushed dried leaves
2 *tablespoons finely minced chives*
2 *tablespoons finely minced fresh parsley*

In a small bowl beat the butter until creamy. Add the lemon juice slowly while continuing to beat. Add the tarragon, chives and parsley and beat until thoroughly combined.

Pack in a covered container and label with suggested uses— chicken, eggs, fish, steaming vegetables.

HERB BUTTER II
1 *cup butter, softened*
4 *tablespoons finely minced fresh oregano or 2 tablespoons*
   finely crushed dried leaves
2 *tablespoons finely minced fresh basil or 1 tablespoon*
   finely crushed dried leaves
2 *tablespoons finely minced fresh chives*

In a small bowl beat the butter until creamy. Add the oregano, basil and chives, and continue to beat until thoroughly combined.

Pack in a covered container and label with suggested uses—on broiled stuffed tomatoes, a finishing touch to broiled steak and chops.

GARDEN JELLIES AND JAMS

The pride of grandmother's pantry were rows of jellies, crystal clear and shimmery smooth, wrung with care and patience from her jelly bag. They preserved the fruits of the orchard, nourishing the family through the long winter months. Because fruit jellies are abundantly available commercially, today's jelly maker is more likely to capture the fresh harvest of the herb garden, blending different herbs in imaginative unions with already prepared fruit juices.

Such jellied treasures have long been traditional gifts from hearth to hearth, and the creative blending of herb and fruit flavors offers opportunities to delight a hostess on many different occasions. The delicate tones of May Wine Jelly make an apt glaze for any fruit tart. Tarragon Wine Jelly becomes roast chicken or veal as Grape Thyme Jelly enhances the flavor of venison, duck or goose; and Rosemary Citrus dresses a pork roast. Fragrant Geranium Jelly makes a beautiful spread for breakfast toast or afternoon tea.

Here is a group of herb-and-fruit jellies. Their taste depends on the freshness of your herbs, their unfailing success and ease of preparation on commercial pectin. Because the success of jellymaking depends in large part on the ratio of pectin, sugar and acid, maintain the proportions in the following well-tested recipes.

Label all your jars and store in a cool, dry place.

MAY WINE JELLY
 2 cups May wine (see page 93)
 3 cups sugar
 2 large pieces orange peel
 2 tablespoons strained lemon juice
½ 6-ounce bottle liquid pectin
 4 sterilized 6-ounce jelly jars
 paraffin
 4 sprigs woodruff for decoration

Place the wine, sugar, orange peel and lemon juice in a large stainless steel or enamel saucepan. Cook over medium heat, stirring constantly, until the sugar is dissolved. Keep the mixture just under the boil and continue cooking and stirring for another five minutes. Remove from heat and discard orange peel. Add the pectin and mix well. Remove the foam carefully from the top of the jelly mixture and pour into prepared jelly jars.

Heat paraffin according to manufacturer's instructions. Cover jelly with ⅛-inch layer of hot paraffin. When slightly cooled, place a sprig of fresh woodruff on the warm paraffin to decorate and identify each jar. Cover with another thin layer of paraffin. The jelly may take up to two days to set.

TARRAGON WINE JELLY

1 *cup fresh tarragon sprigs or* ⅓ *cup finely crushed dried leaves*
¾ *cup lemon juice*
2 *pieces lemon peel*
1½ *cups sauterne*
4 *cups sugar*
½ *6-ounce bottle liquid pectin*
4 *sterilized 6-ounce jelly jars*
paraffin
4 *sprigs fresh tarragon for decoration*

In a small stainless steel or enamel saucepan place the tarragon, lemon juice, lemon peel. Bring to a boil, remove from heat, cover and let steep 15 minutes. Strain through cheesecloth into a large stainless steel or enamel saucepan. Return to the heat and add the wine and sugar, stirring constantly until the sugar is completely dissolved. Bring to a boil, add the pectin, continue stirring, and let the mixture come to a full rolling boil. Remove at once from the heat. Skim the foam carefully from the top of the jelly and pour into prepared jelly jars.

Heat paraffin according to manufacturer's instructions. Cover jelly with ⅛-inch layer of hot paraffin. When slightly cooled, place a sprig of fresh tarragon on the warm paraffin to decorate and identify each jar. Cover with another thin layer of paraffin.

GRAPE THYME JELLY

1 cup fresh thyme sprigs or ⅓ cup finely crushed dried leaves
2 cups bottled grape juice
3 large pieces lemon peel
3 cups sugar
½ cup honey
3 tablespoons lemon juice
½ 6-ounce bottle liquid pectin
4 sterilized 6-ounce jelly jars
paraffin
4 sprigs fresh thyme for decoration

In a small stainless steel or enamel saucepan place the thyme, grape juice and lemon peel. Bring to a boil, remove from heat, cover, and let steep 15 minutes. Strain through cheesecloth into a large stainless steel or enamel saucepan. Return to the heat and add the sugar, honey and lemon juice and stir until the sugar is completely dissolved. Bring to a boil, add the pectin, and let boil hard for just one minute. Remove from the heat. Skim the foam carefully from the top of the jelly and pour into prepared jelly jars.

Heat paraffin according to manufacturer's directions. Cover the jelly with ⅛-inch layer of hot paraffin. When slightly cooled, place a sprig of fresh thyme on the warm paraffin to decorate each jar and cover with another thin layer of paraffin.

ROSEMARY CITRUS JELLY

¾ *cup fresh rosemary sprigs or* ⅓ *cup finely crushed dried leaves*

2 *cups canned unsweetened grapefruit juice*

2 *large pieces orange peel*

2 *tablespoons lemon juice*

3 *cups sugar*

1 *cup honey*

½ *6-ounce bottle liquid pectin*

4 *sterilized 6-ounce jelly jars*

paraffin

4 *sprigs fresh rosemary for decoration*

In a small stainless steel or enamel saucepan place the rosemary, grapefruit juice and orange peel. Bring to a boil, remove from heat, cover, and let steep 15 minutes.

Strain through cheesecloth into a large stainless steel or enamel saucepan. Return to the heat and add the lemon juice, sugar, and honey, and stir until the sugar is completely dissolved. Bring to a boil, add the pectin, and let boil hard for just one minute. Remove from the heat. Skim the foam carefully from the top of the jelly and pour into the prepared jelly jars.

Heat the paraffin according to manufacturer's directions. Cover the jelly with ⅛-inch layer of hot paraffin. When slightly cooled, place a sprig of fresh rosemary on top of the paraffin to decorate each jar and cover with another thin layer of paraffin.

FRAGRANT GERANIUM JELLY

1 cup firmly packed fragrant geranium leaves (rose, lemon, lime, or nutmeg geranium)
2 large pieces lime peel
2 cups bottled apple juice
3 ½ cups sugar
2 tablespoons lime juice
a few drops of red food coloring
½ 6-ounce bottle liquid pectin
4 sterilized 6-ounce jelly jars
paraffin
4 fresh geranium leaves for decoration

In a small stainless steel or enamel saucepan place the geranium leaves, lime peel and apple juice. Bring to a boil, remove from heat, cover, and let steep 15 minutes.

Strain through cheesecloth into a large stainless steel or enamel saucepan. Return to the heat and add the sugar, lime juice and enough food coloring for a pretty rose shade. Stir until the sugar is completely dissolved. Bring to a boil, add the pectin, and let boil hard for just one minute. Remove from the heat. Skim the foam carefully from the top of the jelly and pour into the prepared jelly jars.

Heat the paraffin according to manufacturer's directions. Cover the jelly with ⅛-inch layer of hot paraffin. When slightly cooled, place a fresh geranium leaf on top of the paraffin to decorate each jar and cover with another thin layer of paraffin.

BASIL TOMATO JELLY

1 cup fresh basil leaves or ½ cup finely crushed dried leaves
1¾ cup tomato juice
½ cup strained lime juice
4 cups sugar
½ 6-ounce bottle liquid pectin
4 sterilized 6-ounce jelly jars
paraffin
4 fresh basil leaves for decoration

In a small stainless steel or enamel saucepan place the basil and tomato juice. Bring to a boil, remove from heat, cover, and let steep 15 minutes.

Strain through cheesecloth into a large stainless steel or enamel saucepan. Return to the heat and add the lime juice and sugar, stirring until the sugar is completely dissolved. Bring to a boil, add the pectin, and let boil hard for just one minute. Remove from the heat. Skim the foam carefully from the top of the jelly and pour into the prepared jelly jars.

Heat the paraffin according to manufacturer's directions. Cover the jelly with ⅛-inch layer of hot paraffin. When slightly cooled, place a fresh basil leaf on top of the paraffin to decorate each jar and cover with another thin layer of paraffin.

ROSE HIP JELLY

Rose hips are the fruit of the rose bush, bright orange and red berries that appear in early fall after the petals have fallen from the uncut roses. You must leave some roses on the bush in order for the hips to develop.

Tart and tasty, rose hips are an excellent source of vitamin C, and were used during the Battle of Britain to keep soldiers and civilians alike in good health.

Gather rose hips through the fall, remove the blossom ends and any remaining stem. Wash them thoroughly and keep in an airtight container in the refrigerator until ready to use.

2 quarts fully ripe rose hips to yield 2 cups rose hip juice
water
6 ripe medium tart apples to yield 3 cups apple juice, or
*   3 cups commercial apple juice*
1 tablespoon whole allspice
2 sticks cinnamon
2 large pieces orange peel
1 box dry pectin
several drops red food coloring
6 cups sugar
7 sterilized 6-ounce jelly jars
paraffin

In a stainless steel or enamel saucepan place the prepared rose hips and cover with water. Bring to a boil, then cook over medium-low heat about one hour, until the hips are thoroughly cooked and soft.

Pour cooked hips through a dampened jelly bag or large piece of cheesecloth. Measure 2 cups of the juice into a large stainless steel or enamel saucepan and set aside.

Cut apples into small pieces without peeling or coring them. In a stainless steel or enamel saucepan place the prepared apple pieces, allspice, cinnamon and orange peel, and cover with water. Bring to a boil and simmer until thoroughly cooked and soft. Pour the cooked apples and spices into the jelly bag or large piece of cheesecloth. Measure 3 cups of apple juice and add to the rose hip juice. Add the powdered pectin to the mixture and stir thoroughly. Place over medium-high heat and add food coloring, stirring until the mixture comes to a hard boil. Add the sugar immediately and continue stirring until the mixture comes to a full rolling boil. Let boil hard for one minute only, stirring constantly, then remove from the heat. Skim the foam from the top of the jelly and pour into the prepared jelly jars.

Heat the paraffin according to manufacturer's directions. Cover the jelly with ⅛-inch layer of hot paraffin.

ROSE PETAL PRESERVE
3 cups red rose petals, washed
1½ cups apple juice
2 tablespoons lime juice
rind of 1 lime, grated
3 cups sugar
1 box dry pectin
5 sterilized 6-ounce jelly jars

Snip the white heels from the rose petals. Place petals in a blender, add ½ cup of the apple juice and the lime juice and rind. Process on medium speed until the rose petals are finely chopped.

In a stainless steel or enamel saucepan combine the sugar and remaining cup of apple juice. Heat and stir until the sugar is completely dissolved. Bring to a boil, add the pectin, and let boil hard for one minute only, then remove from heat. Add to the rose petals in the blender and process until thoroughly combined. Pour into the prepared jelly jars and cap tightly. Preserves will keep several weeks in refrigerator.

ROSE PETAL SAUCE

2 quarts rose petals, washed
½ cup orange juice
½ cup water
1 ½ cups sugar
½ cup honey
4 sterilized 6-ounce jelly jars

Snip the white heels from the rose petals and blanch petals in boiling water in a large kettle for one minute. Strain the petals and set aside.

In a saucepan make a syrup of the orange juice, water, sugar and honey. When it comes to a boil, add the petals and simmer until the mixture thickens. Pour into prepared jars, and cap tightly. Sauce will keep several weeks in refrigerator.

DRIED HERBS

One of the nicest and easiest ways to extend your garden bounty is to dry your herbs, then share them with friends. You'll be providing that rarest of treasures for the spice shelf—really fresh-dried herbs.

HERBS FOR DRYING. Most, but not all, of the herbs you enjoy cooking with can be dried with great success. Following is a list of the most common ones:

basil	*lemon verbena*	*rosemary*
catnip	*marjoram*	*sage*
chervil	*mint*	*summer savory*
dill	*oregano*	*tarragon*
lemon balm	*parsley, especially flat-leafed varieties*	*thyme*

For the best flavor and scent, pick the herbs just after the dew has dried but before the sun bakes out the essential oils. Remove any imperfect leaves, rinse off dirt or insecticide and shake off excess water. You can now dry the herbs either by hanging whole plants by their stems or by stripping off the leaves and drying them on screens. In either case, the herbs are dried by circulating warm air, well out of direct sunlight and dampness. As you work, keep each kind of herb separate and clearly labeled; they look quite different when dried.

Herbs with long stems and small leaves like marjoram, sage, savory, rosemary, mints, horehound and catnip are particularly appropriate for hang drying. Gather them in small bunches and tie their stem ends together in an elastic band which will contract as the stem ends dry and shrink. Tie them upside down on a clothesline or coat hangers. Let them hang free so air can circulate.

If your drying area is at all dusty, protect the bunches of herbs by tying a large paper bag around the leafy end. Punch a few holes in the paper bag to guarantee sufficient air circulation. When the leaves are crisply dried in a week or two, strip them from the stems, removing any excess plant material. Save the stems for fireplace faggots (see Section V).

An alternate method, which can be used for all herbs and is preferred for those with large leaves or very short stems, is to dry the leaves individually on a drying screen. This can be an unused window screen or any piece of mesh or screening propped up on a frame or set on a table over bricks so that air can circulate under and over it. Strip the green leaves from the newly harvested herbs and lay them in a single layer on the drying screen. Turn the leaves frequently until they are dry, which will be in about a week. If the drying area is dusty or windy, protect the drying leaves with a layer of cheesecloth.

If a sudden dampness in the weather threatens herbs already drying—by either method—you can complete the drying process in a cool

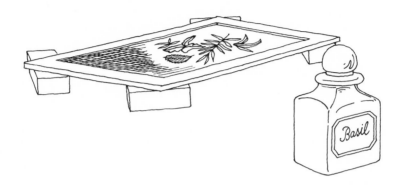

oven, never over 250° F., and preferably between 150 and 200° F. Lay the still-damp leaves out in a single layer on baking sheets, place them in the oven to dry, and leave the door ajar. Remove the leaves just as soon as they are crisp dry. Use oven drying only as a rescue operation; it is a risky method because uneven or over exposure of the leaves can destroy their essential oils.

As soon as the leaves are dry by whatever method you are using, pack them in absolutely airtight containers either whole for teas or crumbled. Label each container. An especially thoughtful personal touch when you give dried herbs away is to include a favorite recipe using the herb.

Mixtures of dried herbs also make delectable gifts. These are various combinations of finely crumbled herbs which impart their distinctive flavor to food. They may be packed loose in tightly stoppered spice jars and added directly during cooking; or as *bouquets garnis*, bagged in cheesecloth for use in the preparation of sauces, soups or stews where the flavor is welcome but the bits of dried foliage are not.

DRIED HERB MIXTURES. For gift giving, try small labeled jars of the following dried herb combinations:

For beef—equal parts thyme, oregano, basil.
For fish—equal parts tarragon, dill, chives, lemon balm.
For eggs and cheese—equal parts chives, marjoram, parsley.
For pork—equal parts sage, basil, summer savory.
For chicken—equal parts tarragon, parsley, marjoram.
For lamb—equal parts marjoram, rosemary, thyme.

BOUQUETS GARNIS. To prepare these herb bouquets, cut 3- or 4-inch squares of muslin or cheesecloth, fill with about 2 tablespoons of mixed dried crumbled herbs. Tie with an extra long thread so the packet can be retrieved from the dish before serving.

Favorite *bouquets* combine 1 generous teaspoon each of dried crumbled herbs in the following combinations:

For beef-based stews, pot roasts or soups—basil, marjoram, parsley, thyme, celery.
For poultry, veal dishes or soups—tarragon, summer savory, dill, parsley, lemon balm.
For cream sauces or soups—parsley, marjoram, celery, thyme.

HERBAL TEAS AND TISANES

Herbal teas or tisanes make exotic brews long invested with curative powers. And while they may not relieve the vapors, malaises or other indispositions, they do make wonderfully aromatic and flavorful infusions. Sip them at bedtime when they seem to work their most soothing magic.

Almost every herb and a few flowers as well can be steeped alone as a tea. Try spearmint, peppermint, lemon balm, lemon verbena, rose geranium, rosemary, sage, bee balm (bergamot), basil, thyme, camomile flowers and rose hips. Blends are also popular: marjoram-mint, lemon thyme-catnip, sage-lemon balm, rosemary-lavender, pineapple mint-bee balm. The fun of tea-making is to use the herbs you grow, either individually or in combination, trying them out in your own garden tea ceremony.

Whatever herb or blends you choose for your infusions, pack the dried whole leaves into tightly capped containers. Include the following directions for brewing with your gift:

Crush whole leaves to release their flavor. Rinse a porcelain (never metal) teapot with hot water to warm it. Using one heaping teaspoon of crushed herbs for each cup of tea, add the herbs loose to the teapot or put them in a caddy. Pour boiling water over the herbs in proper quantity, and let the infusion steep 10 to 15 minutes. A shorter brewing time will make a weaker tea, longer may brew a bitter taste. If you want a stronger brew, add more herbs. And remember to judge the strength of the brew by taste not color, since quick-dried leaves impart a pale green or yellow color and not the ruddy tint of more familiar teas. Herb teas are served with honey or sugar and lemon; milk or cream is not commonly added.

HERB SALTS

There are two ways to make herb salts, one with dried herbs, the other with fresh. Not every herb lends itself to both methods, but in either case, the resulting flavored salt is delicious and makes a wonderfully attractive gift. Package salts in miniature glass-stoppered apothecary jars, tiny Lucite cubes, diminutive stoneware crocks, or recycle empty spice jars and dress them up with charming labels.

DRIED HERB SALTS. Here are five favorite seasoned salts made with dried herbs. For each blend, pound the ingredients together with a mortar and pestle.

FOR POULTRY

¼ *cup non-iodized salt*
 2 teaspoons finely crushed dried lemon balm
 2 teaspoons finely crushed dried tarragon
 2 teaspoons finely crushed dried marjoram

FOR PORK OR POULTRY STUFFING

¼ *cup non-iodized salt*
 2 teaspoons finely crushed dried sage
 2 teaspoons finely crushed dried marjoram
 2 teaspoons finely crushed dried celery leaves

FOR BEEF

¼ *cup non-iodized salt*
 2 teaspoons finely crushed dried thyme
 2 teaspoons finely crushed dried parsley
 2 teaspoons finely crushed dried summer savory
 2 teaspoons finely crushed dried celery leaves

FOR LAMB

¼ *cup non-iodized salt*
 2 teaspoons finely crushed dried rosemary
 1 teaspoon finely crushed dried thyme
 1 teaspoon finely crushed dried lemon balm

FOR SPAGHETTI SAUCE

¼ *cup non-iodized salt*
 1 teaspoon crushed fennel seeds
 2 teaspoons finely crushed dried oregano
 2 teaspoons finely crushed dried basil
 2 teaspoons finely crushed dried parsley

FRESH HERB SALTS. These are made by actually curing the fresh herb in salt, a method of preservation that seems to keep the herb fresher and greener than air drying. It works especially well for dill, basil and tarragon. It has the serendipitous result of transforming the medium into the message; that is, the salt used for the curing process takes on the taste and aroma of the herb.

To make fresh herb salt, place alternate layers of non-iodized salt and fresh herbs in a crock. Cover tightly and put in a cool dark place to cure for several weeks. When the herb is dry, pound the herb and salt together in a mortar and pestle to release the flavor and bottle in a tightly stoppered labeled jar.

MARI-GOLD DUST

Some flowers have a natural affinity for the kitchen, and marigold is one of them. Long popular with cooks, both fresh and dried marigolds have been used for centuries to flavor and color soups, stews, baked goods, and wines. Minced fresh marigold petals can fleck an omelette or chowder with garden sunshine; the dried flowers, which used to be sold by the ounce, are a thrifty substitute for saffron when yellow food coloring is needed for rice and other dishes. Marigolds are a golden gift from the garden all year round.

Wash the marigolds gently, then pick the petals off the blossom and discard the stems and the white heel off each petal. Spread them out on a piece of foil or a baking sheet to dry slowly in a 150–200° F. oven for about two hours. When the petals are thoroughly dry, crumble or pulverize them in a plastic bag with a rolling pin. Pack them in a tightly capped spice jar and label. You may want to include a favorite recipe for bouillabaisse or paella.

SALTED SUNFLOWER SEEDS

Yours for the plucking are the seeds of sunflowers, wild or cultivated. Long before the colonists arrived, American Indians ate them, and today they are a staple in health food stores, revered for their nutritional value and vitamins. They are used like nuts in breads, salads or stuffings, or enjoyed as snacks.

Gather the seeds in early fall when the sun has dried them dark brown or black. Spread them out on a cookie sheet and bake for ten minutes in a preheated 350° F. oven. Now the black shells can be removed easily. Return the shelled seeds to the baking sheet, salt, and oven roast for another ten minutes. Cool in the pan, then package in a sparkling glass jar, in a decorated tin box, or any other pretty container.

PLANTS TO GROW FOR CULINARY DELIGHTS

angelica	*dill*	*oregano*
basil	*elder*	*parsley*
bee balm (bergamot)	*geraniums, fragrant*	*rose*
borage	*horehound*	*rosemary*
camomile	*lemon balm*	*sage*
carnation	*lemon verbena*	*summer savory*
catnip	*lilac*	*sunflower*
chervil	*marigold*	*tarragon*
chives	*marjoram*	*thyme*
dandelion	*mints*	*violet*
day lily	*nasturtium*	*woodruff*

SOURCES OF SUPPLIES

If you cannot find supplies locally or locate them through the classified telephone directory, here are a few sources for mail order shopping. Some sources have catalogs for which there is sometimes a charge.

Bottles

Bathsheba's Bottle Barn, P.O. Box 1776, Millville, N.J. 08332
Greek Island Ltd., 215 E. 49 St., New York, N.Y. 10017
Jim's Bottle Shop, 84 Main St., Dobbs Ferry, N.Y. 10522

Herb stock

Caprilands Herb Farm, North Coventry, Conn. 06238
Cook's Geranium Nursery, 712 North Grand, Lyons, Kan. 67554
Hemlock Hill Herb Farm, Litchfield, Conn. 06759
Hilltop Herb Farm, Box 866, Cleveland, Texas 77327
Shirley Morgan, 2042 Encinal Ave., Alameda, Calif. 94501
Nichols Garden Nursery, 1190 Pacific Highway, Albany, Ore. 97321
Pine Hills Herb Farm, Box 307, Roswell, Ga. 30073
Sunnybrook Farms Nursery, 9448 Mayfield Road, Chesterland, Ohio 44026

Labels

The Herb Farm Country Store, 380 North Granby Rd., Route 189, North Granby, Conn. 06060
Miles Kimball, Bond St., Oshkosh, Wis. 54901

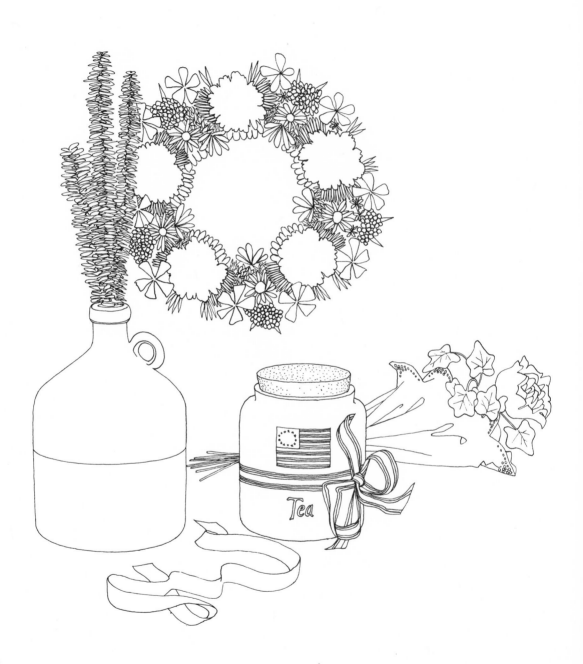

V

GIFTS
FOR ALL SEASONS

Gift giving traditionally marks holidays and special occasions during the year, but for gardeners, never bound by the official calendar, gift giving is year round. Thinning, pruning, dividing, transplanting, they often have an overabundance of botanical stock to split with friend and neighbor. It's a lovely custom, as healthy for the plants as for the friendships.

Making such garden bounty giftworthy is simple. You can do it easily by the addition of a charming container or a special selection of plants to appeal to the interests and tastes of your friends. For example, as your bedding plants come indoors at the end of the season, present some in pots lined up in a French bread basket. Divide some of your herbs and tuck them into the pockets of a strawberry jar. Thin your bulbs or perennials and pack in a watering can. Bring the forced branches of forsythia and other flowering shrubs to friends in a recycled gallon wine jug. Give rooted cuttings of admired plants in a ceramic animal planter. Dress up all your greens in hanging baskets, crocks, pots, planters and any other sort of container that puts a new face on an old friend.

The special selection of plants is another way to customize a garden gift. If there is a bartender on your list, give him pots of various mints for his drinks and a woodruff plant for his May wine. For a chef, plant a mushroom basket with the herbs to season the stuffing of a holiday bird: sage, savory, lemon verbena, parsley. Any cook would be charmed with a selection of the herbs needed for preparing teas, *bouquets garnis*, vinegars or butters. If you know an Elizabethan history fan, plant a wicker clothes hamper with some of the herbs that grew in Shakespeare's garden—marjoram, parsley, savory, mints, lavender, thyme—or enchant him with a bouquet of some flowers that bloomed in the Hampton Court gardens of Elizabeth I—roses, violets, primroses, sweet william.

Saying it with flowers can be even more personal if you send your messages in the very specific language of flowers. For centuries florigraphy has been used to convey intimate unspoken messages. The Chinese and Japanese sometimes conducted affairs of state in this way, as the English, with typical British reserve, conducted affairs of the heart. It may be the nicest romance language; it is certainly the easiest to learn.

With an eye on the lexicon which follows, pick a bouquet or arrange a floral composition which will convey your very personal message.

beauty of mind	clematis
be comforted	geranium
be mine	four-leaf clover
boldness	pink
celibacy	bachelor's button
cheerful	coreopsis
compassion	balm
courage	borage, thyme
declaration of love	tulip
delicate feelings	verbena
esteem	sage
eternal love	heliotrope
faithfulness	forget-me-not
festivity	parsley
fidelity, marriage	ivy
forsaken	anemone
friendship	acacia
grief	marigold
happiness	lily of the valley, marjoram
health	horehound
innocence	white daisy
levity	larkspur
love	rose
loyalty	violet
modesty, innocence	white violet
never-ending remembrance	everlasting
patience	camomile
patriotism	nasturtium
purity	lily, lily of the valley
remembrance	rosemary

repentance	rue
silence	white rose
sorrowful	purple hyacinth
sports, games	blue hyacinth
sympathy	balm, elder
thinking of you, thoughts	pansy
thoughts of absent friends	zinnias
unfading love	globe amaranth
unrequited love	marigold
virtue	mint
wisdom	blue salvia, mint
anger, hostility	tansy
cruelty	nettle
faithlessness, infidelity	daisy
jealousy	yellow rose
malevolence	lobelia
mistrust	lavender

An Englishman sent floral messages to his true love by way of an old fashioned nosegay or bouquet called a tussie mussie. Traditionally, it was a cluster of flowers and leaves held in a filigree holder; later the flowers were simply edged with white lacy paper and tied with a colored ribbon. The central flower, often a rose, carried the main message and was surrounded by other sentiments, perhaps rosemary for remembrance, ivy for fidelity. In *Hamlet*, Ophelia put together a less happy bouquet: rosemary for remembrance, pansies for thoughts, rue for repentance, daisy for faithlessness.

For gift-giving gardeners, florigraphy is an intriguing language, easily transposable from fresh to dried flowers, appropriate for every kind of message. For a sick friend, for instance, surround a cluster of coreopsis (cheer) with balm (sympathy) and horehound (health). Send a new mother a bouquet of red roses (love) surrounded by white daisies (innocence) and blue salvia (wisdom).

Or use your flowers as the most civilized way of expressing your displeasure; who but a florigrapher would know that an appealing bouquet of lavender and tansy actually connotes your mistrust and hostility, or that a bunch of yellow roses signals your jealousy rather than your affection.

As Alice learned in *Through the Looking-Glass*:

"We *can* talk," said the Tiger-lily, "when there's anybody worth talking to."

"And can *all* the flowers talk?"

"As well as *you* can," said the Tiger-lily. "And a great deal louder."

There seem to be certain times when flowers do talk louder, particular holidays that call for celebration by gifts from the garden. Here is a gallery of some of those occasions. As each approaches, look over your supply of botanical treasures—dried, pressed, aromatic, culinary, green and growing—and see how you can transform them to reflect the interests and tastes of the people you like to please.

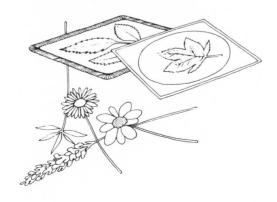

TIMETABLE FOR GIFT GIVING

NEW YEAR'S DAY

POMANDER BALLS

For centuries pomanders have been traditional New Year's gifts, although in their original guise they were far grander than the clove-studded fruits of today. Initially, pomanders were beautiful cases of gold, silver, ivory or china, often encrusted with jewels and powdered gold, and packed with aromatic mixtures whose scents wafted through the apertures of the case to ward off disease, it was believed, or at least to mask the foul odors of unsanitary towns. They were hung from a chain around the neck or waist and worn as much for their antiseptic properties as for their extraordinary beauty. Belief in their health-giving qualities was so widespread that Queen Elizabeth I was said to have always worn a girdle with a pomander, and Cardinal Wolsey to have often carried a hollowed orange or apple filled with spices, which more closely resembles the pomander we know today.

Precious metals and imported spices were too costly for most people, so in time pomanders came to be made of more modest materials—an orange or other fruit stuck with cloves and bathed in spices and fixatives—which, it was devoutly hoped, would be just as effective in keeping its wearer healthy.

You can make your pomanders of oranges, apples, lemons or limes. The fruit should be unblemished, perfectly shaped and thick-skinned. Stud the surface evenly and closely with cloves, turning the fruit so the cloves form a tight, neat "coat of mail" that practically hides its skin. Once you have started making a pomander, don't leave it half finished lest it get hard.

When the fruit has been completely studded with cloves, lay it in an open bowl in a pomander spice mixture made of equal parts of powdered orris root and cinnamon or allspice. Each piece of fruit will require one to two tablespoons of the spice mixture. Turn the pomanders daily in the spices until they are completely cured. The pulp will dry slowly, the juices will seep out and mingle with the ground spices, the skin will shrink, and when the process is completed, the pomander will be dry, light and marvelously aromatic.

Pomander balls are traditionally tied with decorative ribbon and hung around the house. If you are decorating a Christmas tree, hang them toward the trunk of the tree because they are too heavy for the outer branches. On New Year's Day give pomander balls from your tree to visiting guests.

Or use pomanders as placecard holders, tucking the names of your guests between the cloves or flagging them on toothpicks or florist picks. Give them to your holiday dinner guests as yuletide favors.

Or coordinate a pomander ball with another gift, perhaps looping it around the neck of a decorative padded hanger or a hat rack to make a fragrant and useful addition to the hall closet.

Or, in a return to more elegant pomander cases, buy a prettily decorated and perforated china ball in which to put your favorite potpourri mixture.

VALENTINE'S DAY

A PRESSED FLOWER VALENTINE

Hearts and flowers—literally—carry the nicest Valentine sentiments. Pressed posies, particularly when chosen for their floral messages, are appropriate and charming arranged in a heart shape on the inside page of a folded note paper and combined with pressed foliage and lacy paper. Or use the graceful tendrils of a vine to outline the edges of a heart-shaped piece of red construction paper. Cut the paper to fit a ready-made envelope. If you make your valentine more than a few days before you send it, spray the pressed plants with clear lacquer so they will not absorb moisture.

Follow techniques for pressed flower compositions described in Section II.

EASTER

SPRING BULBS

Long before the ground hog emerges to check his shadow, the knowing gardener is enjoying spring indoors with the glorious colors of forced bulbs. Sharing the delights of narcissi, tulips, hyacinths with a friend only requires some advance planning in the preceding autumn.

Plant bulbs for gift giving about four months before the occasion, for example, in early October for Valentine's Day and at Thanksgiving for Easter. Prepare flower pots with shards of clay for drainage and enough soil to fill. A six-inch-diameter pot can accommodate about four daffodils or hyacinths, half a dozen tulips, or a dozen blue grape hyacinths; a four-inch pot will hold about three daffodils or hyacinths, four tulips, and about eight grape hyacinths.

Plant bulbs shallowly, tip up, and water thoroughly. After a few days at room temperature, move the pots to a cool dark place where the temperature can be held to about 45° F.—the refrigerator, basement window, perhaps your garage—and leave the pots for about three months until they develop strong root systems. Then move them into a slightly warmer, slightly lighter environment for a week or so to accustom them gradually to the real world. At this point their leaves have sprouted and they are giftworthy, ready to bask in the sunny window of a friend.

APPLEMINT JELLY

Mints in all their variety are harbingers of spring as well as note-worthy accompaniments to holiday lamb. Both those reasons commend this jelly for Easter giving.

> 1½ *cups firmly packed fresh mint leaves or* ¾ *cup dried*
>   *crumbled leaves*
> 2 *large pieces lemon peel*
> 2 *cups bottled apple juice*
> 3½ *cups sugar*
> 2 *tablespoons lemon juice*
> *green food coloring*
> ½ *6-ounce bottle liquid pectin*
> 4 *sterilized 6-ounce jelly jars*
> *paraffin*
> 4 *fresh mint leaves*

In a small stainless steel or enamel saucepan place the mint leaves, lemon peel and apple juice. Bring to a boil. Remove from heat, cover, and let steep 15 minutes.

Strain through cheesecloth into a large stainless steel saucepan. Return to heat. Add the sugar, lemon juice and food coloring, and stir until the sugar is dissolved completely. Bring to a boil, continue stirring, and add the liquid pectin. Allow the mixture to boil hard for one minute only. Remove from the heat. Skim the foam carefully from the jelly and pour into prepared jars.

Heat the paraffin according to manufacturer's directions. Cover the jelly with ⅛-inch layer of hot paraffin. When cooled, place a mint leaf on top of the paraffin to decorate each jar and cover with another thin layer of paraffin.

JULY FOURTH

INDEPENDENCE TEA

Soothing qualities of herbal teas have always appealed enormously to the Europeans, but during the Revolution Americans brewed them as a protest, substituting native herbal teas for imported tea in order to avoid the onerous British tax. Bee balm (or bergamot) was one such brew which the colonists learned from the Indians and then named Oswego tea. A secondary herb called loosestrife was another brewed by the ladies of the colonies in protest, defiantly called Liberty Tea in the first American consumer action.

In honor of the American Centennial in 1976, we suggest this blend which we named Independence Tea: equal parts dried applemint, thyme, rosemary and bee balm. Package in stoppered containers and tie with a red, white and blue ribbon.

Follow instructions for drying and steeping herbal teas given in Section IV.

THANKSGIVING

AUTUMN WREATHS

Many of the plants hanging in the drying shed can be combined into festive wreaths to be hung for the Thanksgiving holiday and displayed through the Christmas season. They are particularly nice tucked into a base of Silver King or Silver Queen artemisia.

To form an artemisia wreath gather the plant throughout the early fall and use it fairly quickly, before it has time to dry and stiffen. You can use it freshly cut or semi-dried while it is still pliant. Remove the feathery ends with about three to four inches of stem on each, and set them aside.

Choose a wire florist ring an inch or two smaller than the size of the finished wreath; 10 or 12 inches in diameter is a useful size. Take two large bunches of artemisia and face their stem ends toward each other to make one length of the foliage long enough to completely encircle the wire ring. If the artemisia is not supple enough to bend into a circle, crush the boughs at one- or two-inch intervals. Place the artemisia over the wire ring and anchor it with a piece of thin wire looped over and around the boughs. Hide the wire loops with the feathery sprigs of artemisia you have kept in reserve, inserting the stems into the wires and into the boughs as well.

You can transform this basic wreath into an aromatic bouquet by tucking into its crevices sprigs of lavender, rosemary and thyme; or into a bright garden with dried tansy, yarrow, goldenrod, statice and straw-flowers; or into a *bouquet garni* for a cook with spicy cinnamon sticks, nutmegs and sprigs of favorite herbs; or into a forest floor with nuts and tiny pine cone rosettes. Attach the plant materials into the wreath with thin florist wire, drilling holes in the nuts, nutmegs and wherever neces-sary. Trim with berries, ribbons, bows, whatever delights you. At Caprilands Herb Farm where the artemisia wreaths became famous, they are decorated with herbs and spices or dried rosebuds and lavender.

Follow techniques for drying flowers described in Section I.

FLOWER CANDLESTICKS

Dried strawflowers, bluebonnets and similar multi-petal flowers of small size can be mounted on a hemisphere of Styrofoam to form a delightful candlestick. A pair would cheerfully grace the Thanksgiving table.

Glue the flat side of the Styrofoam to a cardboard base for stability. In the very center of the rounded top, cut a plug out of the Styrofoam with an apple corer. Insert into it a ready-made metal candle holder, or line the hole with heavy foil.

Assemble the dried flowers you want to use on the candlestick. If they have dried on thin wires, cut their metal stems to about one inch; if they have dried on their own stalks, carefully remove the stalks and replace with inch-long wires attached either through the eye of the flower or around its calyx. Plunge the metal wire ends into the plastic hemisphere so that the dried flowers completely cover the Styrofoam, except for the candle holder itself. Fill in any open crevices with small foliage like statice. If the flower heads seem heavy or the Styrofoam starts to crumble at all, dip the ends of the wire into white glue (Sobo or Elmer's Glue-All) before inserting in the Styrofoam.

Follow techniques for drying flowers described in Section I.

CRANAPPLE SAGE JELLY

This jelly melds traditional holiday flavors in a new dress and is an especially fitting accompaniment to the Thanksgiving turkey.

> 1½ *cups fresh sage leaves or ½ cup dried crumbled leaves*
> 2 *large pieces orange peel*
> 12 *cloves*
> 1 *cup bottled apple juice*
> 1 *cup bottled cranberry juice*
> 2 *tablespoons lemon juice*
> 3½ *cups sugar*
> ½ *6-ounce bottle liquid pectin*
> 4 *sterilized 6-ounce jelly jars*
> *paraffin*
> 4 *sage leaves*

In a small stainless steel or enamel saucepan place the sage, orange peel, cloves and apple juice. Bring to a boil. Remove from the heat, cover, and let steep 15 minutes.

Strain through cheesecloth into a large stainless steel saucepan. Return to the heat. Add the cranberry juice, lemon juice and sugar, and stir until the sugar is dissolved completely. Bring to a boil, stir in the liquid pectin, and let boil hard for one minute only. Remove from the heat. Skim the foam carefully from the top of the mixture and pour into prepared jelly jars.

Heat the paraffin according to manufacturer's directions. Cover the jelly with ⅛-inch layer of hot paraffin. When cooled, place a sage leaf on top of the paraffin to decorate each jar and cover with another thin layer of paraffin.

CHRISTMAS

CANDIED ANGELICA STEMS

The very special art of candy and cookie decoration would be severely limited without the lovely pale green stems of candied angelica which provide the edible flower stems and tree trunks on frosted holiday treats. If you grow this perennial, delight a friend with a jar of candied angelica in time for her holiday baking.

3 dozen stalks of angelica
1 tablespoon salt
1 tablespoon white vinegar
water
2 cups sugar
green food coloring
small sterile jar

Cut the ridged stalks of young angelica into 3 ½ - to 4-inch lengths. Wash and strip off the thin outer skin.

In a stainless steel or enamel saucepan mix the salt and vinegar in 1 quart of water and soak the pieces of angelica overnight.

Drain the angelica. Cover with water and simmer until the stems become green, about 15 minutes. Drain again.

Prepare the candying syrup in a heavy saucepan by combining the sugar and 1 cup of water. Bring to a boil and add a few drops of green food coloring. Add the angelica stems and simmer until they are translucent and tender.

Stand the angelica stems upright in a small sterile jar and cover with the sugar syrup. Cap tightly and keep in refrigerator.

CHRISTMAS CARDS

Greeting cards with pressed flower designs are lovely ways to convey holiday messages. The tips of many ferns look uncannily like miniature Christmas trees, making them particularly appropriate. They can be decorated with tiny round flowers to simulate Christmas balls or tiny gold and silver stars.

Buy ready-made envelopes, then cut heavy paper to fit into them. You can plan your greeting as a flat card, or as a folded card with the florage on top or inside. In either case, after it is affixed with glue, spray it with clear lacquer to preserve it; many people like to display their yuletide greetings for several weeks.

Follow techniques for pressed flower compositions described in Section II.

CHRISTMAS TREE ORNAMENTS

Nature lovers will welcome the opportunity to decorate the Christmas tree with ornaments fashioned from the garden. Enchant a friend with a set of Christmas tree decorations in the form of pressed flower compositions. Make them in a variety of shapes—bells, balls, candy canes, stars or even in the shapes of roses, daisies, sunflowers—cut out of heavy red cardboard or construction paper. On both sides assemble simple and handsome botanical compositions and insert the cardboard between two pieces of transparent self-adhesive plastic sheeting. Trim the excess film around the edges and punch a hole at the top of each ornament so you can insert a gold or red ribbon for hanging.

Using the same technique, make a wreath of pressed botanicals on a circular piece of cardboard and punch a hole for hanging it from the topmost branch of the Christmas tree.

Follow techniques for pressed flower compositions described in Section II.

The holiday tree is an inviting showcase for all sorts of other unexpected garden products. Consider hanging on the piney boughs a selection of spicy-smelling sachets in holiday shapes: red checked gingham bells on red velvet ribbons, white organdy angels on gold cord. Or calico Raggedy Ann and Andy hanging from sprigs of mistletoe. Pack a selection of seasonal sachets in a red felt Christmas stocking and hang it on a friend's mantel or lay it under the tree.

Follow techniques for sachets described in Section III.

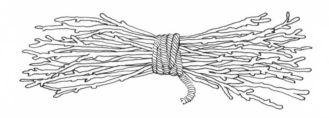

FIREPLACE FAGGOTS

In ancient days the perfumed smoke of burning woods and resins appeased the gods. Later it fumigated sick rooms and warded off disease. Today, dried herbs and sweet woody plants are burned at home solely for their pleasurable fragrance. To this end, collect all the aromatic twigs and woody stems of your dried herbs after pulling off their leaves for potpourris and sachets.

Herbs that yield aromatic faggots include basil, lemon verbena, marjoram, rosemary, savory and thyme. Cut the aromatic stems into pieces of uniform length, perhaps 3 to 6 inches long, and tie them up in small bundles with bright red or green yarn. Keep them in the kindling box for a fragrant winter fire. For your friends, pack the bundles with assorted pine cones in mushroom or small fruit baskets retrieved from the grocer and present as hearthside Christmas gifts.

Follow techniques for drying herbs described in Section IV.

CALENDAR

End your gift-giving year with a calendar of pressed flower compositions. You can make a frame of pressed flowers to surround a small calendar whose pages are torn off as time passes.

Or you can assemble a twelve-page calendar, composing a floral picture to face each monthly page which incorporates in it the botanicals that evoke or are associated with that month—for example, russet leaves facing October, Christmas ferns opposite December, pressed snowdrops facing January.

Follow techniques for pressed flower compositions described in Section II.

SOURCES OF SUPPLIES

If you cannot find supplies locally or locate them through the classified telephone directory, here are a few sources for mail order shopping. Some sources have catalogs for which there is sometimes a charge.

Decorative holiday supplies

Holiday Handicrafts, Inc., Winsted, Conn. 06098

Pomander kits

Caprilands Herb Farm, North Coventry, Conn. 06238
The Herb Farm Country Store, 380 North Granby Rd., Route 189, North
     Granby, Conn. 06060
Hilltop Herb Farm, Box 866, Cleveland, Texas 77327

A GIFTGIVER'S CALENDAR

SPRING

Divide overcrowded perennials like asters, phlox, chrysanthemums and pot for friends.

Divide chive plants, horehound, tarragon and any of the mints and pot for friends.

Gather dandelions for wine.

When flowers open, cut woodruff for May wine.

Pick roses as they bloom for fragrant and culinary gifts.

SUMMER

Cut flowers and herbs for drying as they become ready.

Plant fast-growing annuals to fill out dried flower stock for making arrangements.

Make fresh herb and flower culinary products as plants peak.

Make cuttings of herbs to root for gifts, such as mint, lemon balm, rosemary, fragrant geranium.

Make cuttings of bedding plants to root for gifts, such as impatiens, coleus, begonias.

AUTUMN

Continue to cut flowers and herbs for drying.

Collect wild plants to dry along roadsides, fields, ponds and woods.

Before frost, bring in and pot bedding plants and herbs that won't go through the winter, such as coleus, begonia, impatiens, lemon verbena, rosemary, marjoram, fragrant geranium.

Put bulbs in pots for forcing indoors, such as narcissus, hyacinth, tulips.

Begin making dried flower arrangements when house is dry or heat is turned on.

Make potpourris and sachets.

WINTER

Prune evergreens for Christmas decor.

Force bulbs for indoor bloom.

Force branches of forsythia, pussy willow, flowering quince and other flowering shrubs for early indoor bloom.

WHAT TO MAKE OF YOUR GARDEN

PLANT	Dry	Press	Aromatic	Culinary
Acacia	*	*		
Acroclinium	*			
Allium	*			
Anemone	*			
Angelica				*
Anthemis		*		
Anthurium	*			
Armeria (thrift)	*			
Artemisia	*			
Aster	*	*		
Astilbe	*			
Azalea		*		
Baby's Breath	*			
Bachelor's Button	*			
Basil	*		*	*
Bayberry	*			
Bee Balm	*		*	*
Beech	*	*		
Begonia		*		

PLANT	Dry	Press	Aromatic	Culinary
Bells of Ireland	*			
Bittersweet	*			
Black-eyed Susan	*	*		
Borage				*
Boxwood	*			
Bridal Wreath	*			
Browallia		*		
Butter-and-eggs		*		
Buttercup		*		
Calendula	*			
Camelia	*			
Camomile			*	*
Canterbury Bells	*			
Carnations	*			*
Caryopteris	*			
Catalpa Pods	*			
Catnip			*	*
Cattails	*			
Celandine		*		
Chervil				*
Chestnut Tree Burr	*			
Chives				*
Chrysanthemum (annual)	*			
Clematis		*		
Cockscomb (celosia)	*			
Columbine	*	*		
Coral Bells	*	*		
Coreopsis		*		
Cosmos		*		
Cowslip		*		
Crocus		*		
Daffodil		*		
Daisy	*	*		

PLANT	Dry	Press	Aromatic	Culinary
Dandelion				*
Day Lily				*
Delphinium	*	*		
Deutzia	*			
Dill				*
Dock	*			
Dogwood	*			
Dusty Miller	*	*		
Elder				*
Eucalyptus	*			
Evening Primrose		*		
Ferns		*		
Freesia		*		
Geranium		*		
Geranium, fragrant			*	*
Globe Amaranth	*			
Globe Thistle	*			
Goldenrod	*	*		
Grasses		*		
Heartsease		*		
Heather	*	*		
Helleborc	*			
Holly	*			
Hollyhock	*			
Honesty	*			
Honey Locust Pods	*			
Honeysuckle		*		
Horehound				*
Horse Chestnut Tree Burr	*			
Hydrangea	*	*		

PLANT	Dry	Press	Aromatic	Culinary
Impatiens		*		
Iris Pods	*			
Ivy	*	*		
Joe-Pye Weed	*			
Johnny-jump-ups		*		
Lady's Thumb	*			
Lamb's Ears	*			
Larkspur	*			
Laurel	*			
Lavender	*		*	
Leaves, various		*		
Lemon Balm			*	*
Lemon Verbena			*	*
Liatris	*			
Lilac	*			*
Lily of the Valley	*	*		
Lotus	*			
Love-in-a-mist	*			
Magnolia	*			
Maple Leaves	*	*		
Marigold	*			*
Marjoram			*	*
Milkweed Pods	*			
Mimosa		*		
Mints			*	*
Monkshood		*		
Mullein	*			
Mountain Sage	*			
Nandina Berries	*			
Narcissus		*		
Nasturtium				*

PLANT	Dry	Press	Aromatic	Culinary
Oak Leaves	*	*		
Oregano				*
Palm Foliage	*			
Pansy	*	*		
Parsley				*
Pearly Everlasting	*			
Pennyroyal	*		*	
Peonies	*			
Phlox		*		
Poplar Leaves	*	*		
Poppy		*		
Primrose		*		
Pussywillow	*			
Pyracantha Berries	*			
Queen Anne's Lace	*	*		
Redbud (Judas Tree)	*			
Rhododendron	*			
Rose	*	*	*	*
Rosemary			*	*
Rose of Sharon Pods	*			
Sage			*	*
Sagebrush	*			
Salvia Farinacea (Blue)	*			
Saxifrage		*		
Scabiosa	*	*		
Scilla (Wood Hyacinth)	*			
Snapdragon	*			
Snow-on-the-mountain	*			
Southernwood			*	
Statice	*	*		

PLANT	Dry	Press	Aromatic	Culinary
Strawflower	*			
Sumac	*			
Summer Savory			*	*
Sunflower		*		*
Sweet Gum	*			
Sweet Pea	*			
Tamarisk	*			
Tansy	*		*	
Tarragon				*
Teasel	*			
Thyme			*	*
Trifolium		*		
Trillium		*		
Verbena	*	*		
Violet	*	*		*
Wild Bergamot	*			
Wildflowers, various		*		
Woodruff			*	*
Wood.Sorrel (Oxalis)		*		
Wormwood			*	
Xeranthemum	*			
Yarrow	*			
Yucca Pods	*			
Zinnia	*			

Index